# The Undiscovered Jesus

# The Undiscovered Jesus

## Jesus

HIDDEN TRUTHS FROM THE BOOK OF LUKE

## TIM CROSBY

**Pacific Press®**
Publishing Association
Nampa, Idaho | Oshawa, Ontario, Canada
www.pacificpress.com

Cover design by Review and Herald® Design Center
Cover design resources from Lars Justinen
Inside design by Kristin Hansen-Mellish

Edited by Gerald Wheeler

The author assumes full responsibility for the accuracy of all facts and quotations as cited in this book.

You can obtain additional copies of this book by calling toll-free 1-800-765-6955 or by visiting http://www.adventistbookcenter.com.

Unless otherwise noted, Scripture quotations are from the King James Version.
Scripture quotations marked ESV are from *The Holy Bible,* English Standard Version®, copyright © 2001 by Crossway Bibles, a division of Good News Publishers. Used by permission. All rights reserved.
Texts credited to HCSB are taken from the *Holman Christian Standard Bible,* copyright © 1949, 2000, 2002, 2003 by Holman Bible Publishers. Used by permission.
Scriptures credited to NCV are quoted from *The Holy Bible, New Century Version,* copyright © 2005 by Thomas Nelson, Inc. Used by permission.
Scripture quotations credited to NIV are from the HOLY BIBLE, NEW INTERNA-TIONAL VERSION. Copyright © 1973, 1978, 1984, 2011 by Biblica, Inc. Used by permission. All rights reserved worldwide.
Texts credited to NKJV are from the New King James Version. Copyright © 1979, 1980, 1982 by Thomas Nelson, Inc. Used by permission.
Scripture quotations marked NLT are taken from the *Holy Bible,* New Living Translation, copyright © 1996, 2004, 2007 by Tyndale House Foundation. Used by permission of Tyndale House Publishers, Inc., Carol Stream, Illinois 60188. All rights reserved.
Bible texts credited to NRSV are from the New Revised Standard Version of the Bible, copyright © 1989 by the Division of Christian Education of the National Council of the Churches of Christ in the U.S.A. Used by permission.

ISBN 13: 978-0-8163-5767-3
ISBN 10: 0-8163-5767-6

January 2015

# Contents

# CHAPTER 1

# Born in a Barn?

Luke is the most prolific writer in the Christian canon. No one else wrote as much of the New Testament as he did. Not Paul, not John. A well-educated physician and a native of Antioch, Luke wrote a two-part history of the early church, part 1 (his Gospel) and part 2 (The Acts) in polished Koine Greek. Some have suggested that he was Paul's *amanuensis,* or secretary, for the Pastoral Epistles (see 2 Tim. 4:11). Paul evidently gave him some freedom in choosing the wording, because the Greek there is rather "Luke-like." Early Christian statements also imply that he had some role in the book of Hebrews.

Luke and Acts are addressed to "most excellent Theophilus," evidently a person of status in the Roman Empire. We do not know for sure who he was, but through the centuries people have suggested several identities for Theophilus: one of two Jewish high priests, by that name; Titus Flavius Sabinus II, an older brother of the Roman emperor Vespasian; or Paul's lawyer during his Roman trial. But these are unlikely, as Theophilus was no pagan. "Luke explicitly mentions his having been 'catechized' (*katechethes*, Luke 1:4). This expression means that Theophilus had already received the normal basic instruction given within the Christian Church (1 Cor. 14:19; Gal. 6:6)."[1] In this way he was like Apollos, who also was "catechized" by Priscilla and Aquila (Acts 18:25).

In Eastern Orthodox tradition (which is as ancient as Roman Catholic tradition) Theophilus was the governor, or proconsul, of Achaia, of which the capital was Corinth; a later successor to the Gallio mentioned in Acts 18:12. But most likely he was a wealthy Christian citizen of Antioch, where Luke grew up, who provided financial support for Paul and Luke on their missionary journeys.

In Luke 1:1-4 Luke claims to be a historian. He did not base his books on visions, just good research. Yes, God can even inspire historians! And Luke was a careful one. He did his job with an excellence worthy of his noble cause.

Sir William Mitchell Ramsay (1851-1939) was a British archaeologist who served as a professor at Oxford University and then the University of Aberdeen. As a young man he spent years preparing for an exploratory expedition into Asia Minor and Palestine with the purpose of debunking New Testament history. An adherent of the Tübingen school of scholarship, he believed Acts was second-century fiction. To prove it, he decided to retrace the journeys of Paul, using the book of Acts as a guide.

But his topographical studies in Asia Minor confirmed the full accuracy of the book of Luke's customs, geography, and official titles. Ramsay claims that Luke's references to 32 countries, 54 cities, and nine islands within the book of Acts contain no mistakes. "The narrative" of Acts, he writes, "never makes a false step amid all the many details, as the scene changes from city to city."[2] Again: "Luke is a historian of the first rank; not merely are his statements of fact trustworthy; he is possessed of the true historic sense; he fixes his mind on the idea and plan that rules in the evolution of history; and proportions the scale of his treatment to the importance of each incident. . . . In short, this author should be placed along with the very greatest of historians."[3]

"I take the view," Ramsay said, "that Luke's history is unsurpassed in regard to his trustworthiness. . . . You may press the words of Luke in a degree beyond any other historian's and they stand the keenest scrutiny and the hardest treatment."[4]

More recently, A. N. Sherwin-White said of Acts: "The historical framework is exact. In terms of time and place the details are precise and correct. . . . The feel and tone of city life is the same as in the descriptions of Strabo and Dio of Prusa. . . . The detail is so interwoven with the narrative of the mission as to be inseparable."[5]

Still more recently Colin J. Hemer provided extensive evidence of Luke's accuracy.[6]

* * *

Luke specializes in the Christmas story. No other writer tells us so much about it as he did. One of his sources was no doubt Mary herself (see Luke 2:19). Her famous account includes a big surprise for us. Contrary to long-standing tradition, Jesus was not born in some stable attached to an inn. No, he was born in a private home. I am sorry to ruin hundreds of Christmas plays by telling you this. But I do my best to be a careful researcher too. And I have to report what I (and many other scholars) have found.

It all started this way. God sent Gabriel to the priest Zechariah to tell him his wife would have a child (Luke 1:5-17, NIV). Then, "in the sixth month of Elizabeth's pregnancy, God sent the angel Gabriel to Nazareth, a town in Galilee, to a virgin pledged to be married to a man named Joseph, a descendant of David. The virgin's name was Mary. The angel went to her and said, 'Greetings, you who are highly favored! The Lord is with you.' Mary was greatly troubled at his words and wondered what kind of greeting this might be" (Luke 1:26-29, NIV).

*Whatever could Gabriel want,* Mary must have thought, *with little me?* The last time he showed up in Scripture was to Daniel, whom Gabriel said was "highly esteemed" (Dan. 9:21-23, NIV). Now Gabriel is saying the same of Mary. And heaven does not indulge in flattery. It was all too much, terrifying in its implications.

"Do not be afraid, Mary," the angel continued. "You have found favor with God" (Luke 1:30, NIV). "Fear not" is the most common command in the Bible. In Scripture God or His messenger tells this to various chosen people approximately 100 times! When God sends a message to human beings, it is most likely to begin with "Don't be afraid."

Gabriel went on: "You will conceive and give birth to a son, and you are to call him Jesus. He will be great and will be called the Son of the Most High. The Lord God will give him the throne of his father David, and he will reign over Jacob's descendants forever; his kingdom will never end" (verses 31-33, NIV).

*Well,* she must have been thinking, *I don't think so! This is beyond belief! How could it be true? You must know something I don't.* "But I'm a virgin!" she said out loud (see verse 34).

Gabriel explained that the Holy Spirit would impregnate her and that her child would be the Son of God (verse 35, NIV).

" 'I am the Lord's servant,' Mary answered. 'May your word to me be fulfilled' " (verse 38, NIV).

She had greater faith when the angel told her something impossible than Zechariah did when God said something merely improbable. Earlier in the chapter He had announced to Zechariah that he and his aged wife would have a child, which Zechariah had been praying for. Yet when his prayer was answered, he wasn't sure whether to believe it or not. A wizened old priest who had seen all sorts of schemes, he was skeptical.

"How can I be sure?" he asked. "We're too old, you know" (see verse 18).

"You want a sign?" the angel replied. "OK—you'll be mute until it happens" (verses 19, 20).

Be careful what you ask for. Zechariah didn't believe God's answer even though he had been praying for it. But Mary—young, naive Mary—had great faith. God said it, and that was good enough for her.

Now what do you suppose she thought after the angel left? *This is the most wonderful news in the world! I'm going to bear the Messiah. I'll be the most honored woman in Israel!* Or was it more like: *This is going to ruin my life! What will people think?* Perhaps it was a mixture of both.

Most teens are obsessed with how others view them. And according to the earliest traditions we have, Mary was only about 14 at the time.

How others regard them is what most Christians worry about much of the time. *What will others think of me if I pray in public or praise out loud or raise my hands? What if I do this or that? What will it do for my career?* Imagine if John the Baptist had worried about what effect his strange way of life would have on his career. Or what if Jesus had decided to avoid saying something so offensive as in Matthew 23:13-39 or John 6:35-66?

Well, from the standpoint of those in charge of Mary, it was a real career buster. So her people bundled her up and sent her away to visit her relative Elizabeth, wife of Zechariah, who had received a similar shock because she herself was suddenly pregnant—despite her old age. That would get Mary out of the community so that people wouldn't know about her condition.

But when the younger woman arrived, still contemplating in awe the news that her son was the promised Messiah, Elizabeth's baby leaped in her womb for joy (verses 39-45).

And then Mary recited what Christian tradition often calls the Magnificat, part of which reads as follows:

> "He has performed mighty deeds with his arm;
> he has scattered those who are proud in their inmost thoughts.
> He has brought down rulers from their thrones
> but has lifted up the humble.
> He has filled the hungry with good things
> but has sent the rich away empty" (verses 51-53, NIV).

God blesses humility and curses arrogance. He brings the low high and the high down low. The Lord fills the hungry with good things but sends the rich away empty. To be blessed by God we have to empty our hands so that He can fill them. For most of us our cup is so full that God can't pour anything into it. Possessing comforts denied to kings in times past, we have so many things to occupy our time that we have no time for God. God wants us to empty ourselves, to make room for Him. To humble ourselves so that He can lift us up.

If you feel empty, you are right on the verge of God's greatest blessing. Just seek His face. Should you be desperate and hurting and experiencing loss, remember that the Lord lifts up the downcast and casts down the proud. He will in His own good time turn your mourning into joy.

* * *

Mary's nine months passed quickly.

About that time Caesar Augustus decreed that "all the world" (i.e., the Roman Empire) should register for a census. We find the date for it in Luke 2:2, which mentions the registration when Quirinius (NIV) was governor of Syria. But the reference has long been a difficult problem, as the census of Quirinius took place in A.D. 7, and we have no explicit record of any previous census by him. As a result, many translations make it appear that Jesus was born during this census, when He should have been about 10 years old. At no point has Luke been more universally attacked than this passage, and many scholars claim it is in error. Here is the acid test of the claim that Luke is a careful historian.

F. M. Heichelheim first discovered a likely solution in 1938. It involves a different translation of Luke 2:2: "This census was *before* the census taken when Quirinius was governor." As the standard lexicons indicate, the Greek word *protos,* when followed by the genitive, can mean "before," as it does in John 1:15, 30; 5:36; 15:18; 1 Corinthians 1:25, and so on.

So Luke is talking about some earlier census *before* the better-known one under Quirinius, which everyone knew about, including Luke (Acts 5:37).

But why did Joseph have to return home? Liberal scholars claim we have little evidence for such a requirement for a Roman census, but absence of evidence is not evidence of absence. Rome may have reasoned that people can be counted only if they go back to their homes, not wandering around in the empire. Even today we have to return to a particular district in order to vote. But we do indeed have evidence for people in the Roman Empire coming home to register.

Early in the twentieth century scholars discovered a papyrus dating from about A.D. 104. It contained an edict by Gaius Vibius Maximus, the Roman governor of Egypt, stating: "Since the enrollment [*apographe,* census—the same word used by Luke] by households is approaching, it is necessary to command all who for any reason are out of their own district to return to their own home, in order to perform the usual business of the taxation."

Some have argued that the requirement mainly concerned migrant workers, but highly respected scholar Raymond E. Brown (1928-1998) suggested that "one cannot rule out the possibility that, since Romans often adapted their administration to local circumstances, a census conducted in Judea would respect the strong attachment of Jews to tribal and ancestral relationships."[7]

We know of a empire-wide census around the time Jesus was born because of "The Deeds of the Divine Augustus," an important inscription on the his mausoleum. Point 8, in the Loeb translation, reads in part: "Three times I revised the roll of the senate. In my sixth consulship, with Marcus Agrippa as my colleague, I made a census of the people. . . . In this lustration 4,063,000 Roman citizens were entered on the census roll [28 B.C.]. A second time, in the consulship of Gaius Censorinus and Gaius Asinius, I again performed the lustrum alone, with the consular imperium. In this lustrum 4,233,000 Roman citizens were entered on the census roll [7 B.C.]. A third time, with the consular imperium, and with my son Tiberius Caesar as my colleague, I performed the lustrum in the consulship of Sextus Pompeius and Sextus Apuleius. In this lustrum 4,937,000 Roman citizens were entered on the census roll [A.D. 15]."

It is possible that this census took several years, because we know that the Senate was revised around A.D. 3. But somewhere between 7 and 3 B.C. the census reached Judea.

Roman registrations normally involved (1) taxation, (2) military service (Jews were exempt), and (3) special government "ballots." Ernest L. Martin lists the evidence that the Romans voted such a registration in 3 B.C.:

There is a reference to such a registration of all the Roman people not long before 5 February 2 B.C. written by Caesar Augustus himself: "While I was administering my thirteenth consulship [2 B.C.] the senate and the equestrian order *and the entire Roman people* gave me the title Father of my Country" (*Res Gestae* 35, italics supplied). This award was given to Augustus on 5 February 2 B.C., therefore the registration of citizen approval must have taken place in 3 B.C. Orosius, in the fifth century, also said that Roman records of his time revealed that a census was indeed held when Augustus was made "the first of men"—an apt description of his award "Father of the Country"—at a time when all the great nations gave an oath of obedience to Augustus (6:22, 7:2). Orosius dated the census to 3 B.C. And besides that, Josephus substantiates that an oath of obedience to Augustus was required in Judea not long before the death of Herod (*Antiquities* 17:41-45).

This agrees nicely in a chronological sense with what Luke records. But more than that, an inscription found in Paphlagonia (eastern Turkey), also dated to 3 B.C., mentions an "oath sworn by all the people in the land at the altars of Augustus in the temples of Augustus in the various districts." And dovetailing precisely with this inscription, the early (fifth century) Armenian historian, Moses of Khoren, said the census that brought Joseph and Mary to Bethlehem was conducted by Roman agents in Armenia where they set up "the image of Augustus Caesar in every temple." The similarity of this language is strikingly akin to the wording on the Paphlagonian inscription describing the oath taken in 3 B.C. These indications can allow us to reasonably conclude that the oath (of Josephus, the Paphlagonian inscription, and Orosius) and the census (mentioned by Luke, Orosius, and Moses of Khoren) were one and the same. All of these things happened in 3 B.C.[8]

Here is my own contribution about the historical situation: Joseph would have had to adopt Jesus as his own child. Even apart from any consideration of forced return, Joseph, believing that Mary's son was to be the promised Messiah, the son of David, may have wanted his son to be born—and adopted—in Bethlehem, the ancestral home of the lineage of David, to fulfill the well-known prophecy (see Matt. 2:4-6) and to protect His right to the throne. Indeed, he may have wanted witnesses to the adoption from his Davidic clan.

So Joseph took Mary to Bethlehem.

\* \* \*

"While they were there, the time came for the baby to be born, and she gave birth to her firstborn, a son. She wrapped him in cloths and placed him in a manger, because there was no guest room available for them" (Luke 2:6, 7, NIV).

Before we talk about the guest room, let's consider the manger. For us the word "manger" invokes a stable or barn. But at Bethlehem, in Jesus' day, the manger was inside every home. Almost everyone in Palestine had a manger in their house unless they were quite wealthy.

Simple village homes in Palestine often had only two rooms, one reserved exclusively for guests. The roof is flat and can have a guest room built on it, or a guest room can be attached to the end of the house. Someone who stayed in a guest room on the roof was Elijah in 1 Kings 17:19.

The main room of the house was one where the entire family cooked, ate, slept, and lived. Jesus assumes such simple homes when He comments: "Neither do people light a lamp and put it under a bowl. Instead they put it on its stand, and it gives light to everyone in the house" (Matt. 5:15, NIV). How can one light shed light on everyone in the house? Because the house in effect has only one room.

The end of the room closest to the door was usually a few feet lower than the rest of the floor, or else it was blocked off with heavy timbers. That area was where the family cow, donkey, and sheep would spend the night. And every morning members of the family would take the animals out, tie them up in the courtyard of the house, and clean the animal stall for the day. They could wash it out now and then because it was lower than the floor of the regular living area.

The farmer wanted his animals inside the house each night because it kept them safe from theft and because they provided heat in the winter.

Luke 13:15 refers to just such an in-home menagerie. Jesus heals a woman with a long infirmity, and the Pharisees get after Him for healing on the Sabbath. So He turns the argument back on them: "You hypocrites! Doesn't each of you on the Sabbath untie your ox or donkey from the stall and lead it out to give it water?" (NIV). "You work on the Sabbath too," He said. "You have mercy on your animals, you lead them out of your house into the yard and provide water for them. You untied an animal this morning, but I untied a daughter of God." And that ended the discussion.

Many Old Testament stories assume such a style of home. For example, in 1 Samuel 28:24 Saul was a guest in the house of the medium of Endor when the king refused to eat. The medium took a fatted calf that was "in the house," killed it, and prepared a meal for the king and his servants. She did not fetch a calf from the field or the barn, but from within the house.

Then there is the story of Jephthah in Judges 11. He made a vow that if God would grant him victory, then he would sacrifice the first thing that came out of his house. When he returned home, to his horror, it was his daughter that stepped first out of the house. Most likely he arrived early in the morning and fully expected one of the animals to come bounding out when released.

Now if we were to draw the outline of a floor plan of such a house, looking down from above, we would see two puzzling circles on the floor. What do they represent? Those are the mangers dug out of the floor. That's where they placed the straw for the animals. The floor in the family living room slopes down slightly toward the animal stall to aid in sweeping and washing. If Bessie the cow gets hungry in the night, she can stand up and eat out of the manger. The sheep may have their own mangers made of wood and placed on the floor of the lower level.

So where was Jesus born? In a private home, which had a manger. But if Jesus was born in a private home and not in a public inn, then why does the King James Version and even some modern versions read, "There was no room for them in the inn" (Luke 2:7), as if the no vacancy sign was on and Jesus had to sleep with the animals?

Well, that is probably not the best translation. What the Greek text says is that there was no *topos* in the *katalyma*. That is, there was no space or room in the *guest quarters*. The NIV translates: "because there was no guest room available for them." How do we know this is correct? By letting Luke define his own words. And the word he uses here is not the one he employs for an inn.

In the parable of the good Samaritan (Luke 10) the Samaritan picks up the wounded man from the side of the road and takes him to an inn. The Greek word in that text is *pandocheion*. Let's break that down. The first part, "pan," means "all," as in Pan-American. The second part means "to receive." The *pandocheion* is the place that "receives all," that is, a commercial inn, a hotel.

If Luke wanted to say that Joseph was turned away from an "inn," he would have used *pandocheion*. But in Luke 2:7 it is the *katalyma* that is crowded. *Katalyma* simply means "a place to stay." It could indicate an inn, or a house, or a guest room. But Luke uses this term only one other place in his Gospel, which gives us a strong hint that he employs it to mean the guest room in a private home.

"He replied, 'As you enter the city, a man carrying a jar of water will meet you. Follow him to the house that he enters, and say to the owner of the house, "The Teacher asks: Where is the guest room [*katalyma*] where I may eat the Passover with my disciples?" He will show you a large room upstairs, all furnished. Make preparations there' " (Luke 22:10-12, NIV).

Now let's take what we have learned and apply it to the Christmas story. Mary and Joseph stop at a private home. The owners can't give them the guest room, but they take them in anyway. And when baby Jesus is born, He was laid in a manger full of soft straw.

Luke's story matches Matthew 2:11, which says Jesus was in a "house" when the magi visited, so evidently the couple stayed for a while.

Joseph had a well-known lineage in Bethlehem, and all he would have had to do is mention his famous forefathers—the ones listed in Luke 3:23-38—and any family in town would have been honored to receive him. He belonged to the kingly clan of Judah. Luke 2:4 says that Joseph went "to Bethlehem the town of David, because he belonged to the house and line of David" (NIV). He was special—he was royalty.

Did he already have reservations with this family? Evidently not, or they would have kept the guest room for them. That's not certain, however, because ancient custom might have required the homeowner to extend hospitality to the first person who asked, and someone else might have come along first. In the biblical world people were obligated to extend hospitality to visiting strangers (see Heb. 13:2).

Did Joseph have to make an emergency stop because Mary was about to give birth? Perhaps. At any rate, some anonymous resident of Bethlehem, possibly a relative, brought Joseph and Mary into their own home in her hour of need and laid their new little Baby in the straw right in the living room, either down in the hole carved out of the rock for the animals, or else they moved a manger full of straw into the living space. They just couldn't put them in the guest room because it was already full. So they gave them what they had.

Is your life already so full that you have no place for Jesus? Have you given Him your best? Have you put Him not just in the periphery of your life, but brought Him right into the center of your existence? Is Jesus your butler in the sky—someone to call on only when you need something—or is He Lord of all?

Have you opened to Him every room of your heart?

Christ, He requires still, wheresoe'er He comes
To feed or lodge, to have the best of rooms:
Give Him the choice; grant Him the nobler part
Of all the house: the best of all's the heart.

—Robert Herrick

1. Patrick Henry Reardon, "Most Excellent Theophilus," *Touhstone,* December 2002, accessed December 2, 2014, www.touchstonemag.com/archives/article.php?id=15-10-026-c.

2. W. M. Ramsay, *St. Paul the Traveller and the Roman Citizen* (London: Hodder and Stoughton, 1897), p. 238.

3. W. M. Ramsay, *The Bearing of Recent Discovery on the Trustworthiness of the New Testament* (Grand Rapids: Baker Book House, 1953).

4. W. M. Ramsay, *Luke the Physician* (London: Hodder and Stoughton, 1908), p. 222.

5. A. N. Sherwin-White, *Roman Society and Roman Law in the New Testament* (Grand Rapids: Baker Book House, 1978), pp. 120-122.

6. Colin J. Homer, *The Book of Acts in the Setting of Hellenistic History* (Winona Lake, Ind.: Eisenbrauns, 1990).

7. Raymond E. Brown, *The Sixth of the Messiah: A Commentary on the Infancy Narratives in the Gospels of Matthew and Luke* (New York: Doubleday, 1993), p. 549.

8. Ernest L. Martin, "The Nativity and Herod's Death," in Jerry Vardaman and Edwin M. Yamauchi, eds., *Chronos, Kairos, Christos: Nativity and Chronological Studies Presented to Jack Finegan* (Winona Lake, Ind.: Eisenbrauns, 1989), pp. 89, 90.

# CHAPTER 2

# Crisis in the Desert

Most of us have never really had to depend on God alone. We have plenty of props, comforts, and diversions around us to use. Few of us have ever had a crisis in which there was really nothing we could do about it, in which all our resources failed, and during which we were at our wits' end and had to rely wholly on divine power.

In order for us to become spiritually mature, in order to jump out of our current reality into the next higher realm of spirituality, we need to find ourselves in a situation in which there seems no way out. We must have all the props knocked out from under us.

As an example, take the time when God delivered Israel from the armies of Egypt. He came to the Hebrews who had grown resigned to the routine of slavery in Egypt and announced, "Get out." Leave your home and go out into the desert—a wildly impractical idea for such a horde. When the Egyptian forces pursued the terrified slaves, God might have wiped the army out early on. Instead He let the Hebrews get cornered between the devil and the "deep blue" sea. They were trapped. Only God could save them. They had no way out but up. Scripture is full of such crises. The Lord seems to enjoy brinkmanship.

I'm told that at a certain point in the life of a young eagle, the mother rips away the soft down of the nest, leaving only the thorns, making the baby bird uncomfortable enough to want to fly away. Well, God does that too. He came to Abraham living in an advanced pagan culture and said, "Get out."

"Where to, Lord?"

"Tell you later."

God told the Jews who had settled down comfortably in Babylon, "Get out. Go back home to the ruins."

To Saul and many others after the Resurrection He said, "Leave your comfortable family of faith with its venerable traditions and join this upstart group, 'the Way,' that they're calling a cult."

To those who were comfortable members of the medieval church He urged, "Get out. Go join these protesters led by Martin Luther."

Next He came to those who had grown comfortable in the churches of the 1840s and invited them to join the new Advent movement. And still He calls, to those living in spiritual Babylon, "Come out of her, my people" (Rev. 18:4).

Each year He leads hundreds of students in Adventist colleges and universities to leave their friends and volunteer as student missionaries in strange new cultures. A mission journey is a transforming experience.

Nothing changed my life as much as my mission trip to the Philippines in 1992 when I worked for the Voice of Prophecy. I landed in the Philippines with no luggage—the airline had lost it—and no one was there to pick me up. So I know just a little bit of what it means to be without resources and have only God.

I distinctly remember thinking, *I wonder what God's gonna do next!*

What is the point of a crisis? One of the things it does is teach us that nothing but God is more than enough. When we learn that, we will never be the same.

Even Jesus needed a crisis. In His case it was 40 days in the desert without food. "Get out. Get away from Your friends and Your support system. Leave Your job. Go wrestle with Me in the desert." Mark says that He was driven into the desert (see Mark 1:12), and not in a Jeep Grand Cherokee. Matthew and Luke, writing later and exerting their editorial prerogative by touching up some things in Mark that they thought might be improved a bit, make it sound a little more gentle: He was *"led"* into the desert (Matt. 4:1; Luke 4:1).

I like "driven" better. Like a leaf swept along by the wind of the Holy Spirit, He was compelled to go there. He heard the call of the wild. Dropping His carpenter's tools and His comfortable income, He left it all behind for what must have seemed to His associates as some crazy quest in the desert.

Jesus had to find out what it meant to be the Son of Man.

That was Jesus' favorite title for Himself. It does not merely emphasize His humanity. Instead, it hides some of the deepest truths of Scripture. The title is derived from Daniel 7, a chapter that provides a major part of the foundation on which Christianity rests. Indeed, Daniel 7 helps us understand what Jesus was doing in the wilderness for 40 days.

Just before we go to Daniel, it is important to mention that the Greek translation of the Hebrew scriptures used by almost everyone in Jesus' day— the "authorized version" in Greek, just as the King James Version was the authorized version in English for several hundred years—was the Septuagint, translated by 70 (or 72) Greek scholars in Alexandria, Egypt, under the ruler Ptolemy Philadelphus, several hundred years before Christ. Philo tells the story in *Life of Moses* (2.25-44).

It is important to know that, whenever the New Testament cites the Old, it is almost always citing the Septuagint.

The Septuagint is abbreviated LXX (the Roman numeral for 70), just as the King James Version is abbreviated KJV. So whenever we cite some Old Testament text followed by "LXX" (such as this: Isaiah 53:4, LXX), that means the Septuagint version in Greek and not the Hebrew. This is important, because the Septuagint helps us to unlock some biblical mysteries.

* * *

Careful students of the Scriptures will notice that many of the Old Testament passages that Jesus applied to Himself arguably refer to Israel as a nation in their original context. So why did He apply them to Himself as a person?

The answer is that Jesus understood the equation between representative and represented. That is—to use modern legal terms to describe a scriptural concept—the principle was a corporation. In other words, Jesus was Israel. He was the Son of man of Daniel 7, both corporately and individually. Let me explain. Put on your thinking caps, because we are in for a bit of a tough slog. But the end result is something wonderful.

In Daniel 7 we find four empires symbolized by four fierce animals (instead of metals as in Daniel 2). The fourth empire, or an extension of it, persecutes the people of God, but a great heavenly court sits in judgment, the persecuting power gets destroyed, and "one like the son of man" (i.e., one of human form, in contrast to the preceding beasts) comes to the Ancient of Days, and He receives eternal dominion (verses 13, 14, NIV). The kingdom of God is the fifth and final empire.

The "Son of man" in Daniel 7 has generated much controversy. Liberal scholars understand him to be a corporate figure representing the people of God, while ancient Christian tradition, as well as Jewish, sees this Son of man as the Messiah. The latter position is, of course, the Adventist one.

Frankly, the text of Daniel offers support for both views.

The evidence for the corporate view is as follows: Like all the prophecies of Daniel, the vision of Daniel 7 divides into two parts: a symbolic vision (Dan. 7:1-14) and an interpretation (verses 16-27). Read it carefully, and you will notice something strange. The Son of man appears only in the symbolic vision, while the saints appear only in the interpretation. That is, in the second half of the prophecy (the explanatory part), the symbolic Son of man has vanished, to be replaced by the literal saints. Whatever happens to the Son of man in the symbolic vision happens to the saints in the interpretation. Obviously, then, the Son of man is a symbol of the saints, the people of God. Just as the four Gentile kingdoms are each symbolized by a symbol that is subhuman (beasts), so God's people are portrayed by a symbol that is human or superhuman.

Scripture refers to the symbolic being as "like" a Son of man—that is, humanlike. The same chapter describes the preceding kingdoms as "like" a lion, "like" a bear, and "like" a leopard, but these are not, in fact, literal animals. The hair of the Ancient of Days is "as" snow and "like" wool but not actually snow or wool. Likewise, then, neither is the Son of man an actual man—he is a symbolic corporate figure representing God's people. The liberal position here makes perfect sense. It is clearly correct.

But wait! Closer inspection of the text reveals something more here than a corporate symbol.

The crucial insight is that the four beasts of Daniel 7 represent not only kingdoms (Dan. 7:23) *but also kings*. Verse 17 says that the four great beasts "are four *kings*." The translation "kingdoms" found here in many versions (starting with the LXX) is not literally correct. The original Aramaic is *melek,* "kings." But the parallel passage in verse 23 reads "kingdoms" because, in Daniel, "king" and "kingdom" are interchangeable—not just here but also in Daniel 2:37-40, in which the head of gold represents Nebuchadnezzar, while the other parts of the image depict "kingdoms." And in Daniel 8:20-22 horns first stand for kings, then kingdoms.

In other words, Daniel's symbolic beasts represent not just kingdoms but also the conquerors who founded the dynasty—Nebuchadnezzar, Cyrus, Alexander, and so on—men who could be called messiahs (Isa. 45:1 labels Cyrus "his anointed"). In the same way, then, "one like the Son of man" represents not only the fifth kingdom but also its conquering king, the Messiah par excellence.

Why does Scripture depict the final king/kingdom by a symbol that is more than a beast? Could it be to suggest that the king is more than a human being? In three other places Daniel sees a glorious being that looks like a man (Dan. 8:15; 10:16, 18). Daniel 8:16 identifies the being with Gabriel. True, this figure is not part of a symbolic vision. Still, whenever Daniel views something in vision that looks "like a man," he is talking about a superhuman being. The terminology originates with a passage in Ezekiel, an older prophet who was in Babylon with Daniel: "High above on the throne was a figure like that of a man" (Ezek. 1:26, NIV). According to scholar William Shea, the passage was written before Daniel 7, even given the conservative, early dating of Daniel.

The Son of man comes riding on the clouds of heaven (Dan. 7:13). Elsewhere only God rides the clouds (Deut. 33:26; Ps. 68:4). Furthermore, the Son of man is the object of worship: "all peoples, nations, and languages should serve him" (Dan. 7:14). The corresponding passage in the interpretation is verse 27, in which the one who is worshiped is not Israel, as we would expect, but God. If the Son of man were nothing more than a corporate symbol representing the saints, then the last sentence of verse 27 should read, "*Their* kingdom will be an everlasting kingdom, and all rulers will worship and obey *them.*" Instead, the object of worship is an individual: "All rulers will worship and obey *him*" (NIV). Scripture uses similar language elsewhere to describe Israel's ideal king: "Endow the king with your justice, O God, the royal son with your righteousness. . . . May he endure as long as the sun, as long as the moon, through all generations. . . . *All kings bow down to him and all nations serve him*" (Ps. 72:1-11, NIV).

The Son of man in Daniel, then, represents the saints in corporate unity with their leader—a leader very much like the child ruler of Isaiah 9:6, 7 called "mighty God" and whose kingdom is forever. Early Jewish writings identify the individual in the passage as the Messiah. The Semitic mind could, without contradiction, understand the symbol as representing both the leader and his followers, just as the priest incorporates those whom they represent in Leviticus 4:3 or Zechariah 3. In other words, the Son of man is a *corporation*—something even the contemporary Western mind can understand—and the Messiah is the president.

Early Jewish tradition identified the Son of man in Daniel with the Messiah. According to Geza Vermes: "Mainstream Jewish interpretative tradition recognized Dan 7:9-14 from the early second century A.D. at least, but almost certainly even earlier, as a Messianic text depicting the coming of the new, glorious, and exalted David."[1] In light of the consensus between Judaism and early Christianity, the attempt on the part of some twentieth-century liberal scholars to limit the meaning of the Son of man to a corporate symbol fails. *The text of Daniel itself supports both interpretations at the same time.*

To sum up: The idea that the "Son of man" in Daniel 7 is a Messianic figure rests on pre-Christian evidence. Yet the Son of man is also a corporate figure that represents the saints. It is a paradox that we must maintain, because it provides us with a critical clue to Jesus' self-concept. If He understood

Daniel's Son of man on both levels—saints and savior—then He could see Himself as Israel.

And if Jesus is a corporation—if the Son of man is the saints—then *whatever happened to the Son of man happened to the saints.* It explains the later Christian understanding of Jesus' death as a vicarious atoning sacrifice. When Jesus is our high priest, and we accept Him as Savior, we join His company. In other words, we are "adopted" and incorporated into Him, become part of His body. Whatever happens to you happens to your body, right? Well, what happens to Jesus happens to us, and vice versa. Can you see how much light this sheds on Paul's favorite expression: "in Christ"? That is how Paul can say, "One died for all, and therefore all died" (2 Cor. 5:14, NIV). When Jesus died, we died. But we're getting ahead of ourselves.

The same pattern of corporate versus individual reality appears in many passages of the Old Testament. For example, we find it in Isaiah 53, the famous "suffering servant" passage that refers not to the Messiah but to the "servant of Yahweh." And who is that? Well, Isaiah 41:8, 9; 43:10; 44:1, 2, 21; 45:4; 48:20; and 49:3 (and even Luke 1:54!) repeatedly and explicitly correlate the servant figure with Israel. So why do we identify it with Jesus? Well, the explanation for Isaiah 53 is the same as for Daniel 7.

We can check out this conclusion by a closer look at Isaiah 49, another "servant of Yahweh" passage that, judging by the many New Testament allusions, was special to Jesus too. It clearly identifies the servant of Yahweh with Israel (verse 3), then just as clearly distinguished the Servant from Israel (verses 4, 5). How could this be? The paradox vanishes, however, if the one represents the many. These are some of the reasons that Jesus, early on, came to the conclusion that *He was Israel.*

OK, but just how is all of this relevant to Jesus' 40-day fast in the desert? Here's where the story gets interesting. As Israel, Jesus apparently felt that it was His task to recapitulate the history of the nation in miniature—and that without sinning (because, remember, if an anointed one, such as the high priest, sins, he brings guilt on the people [see Lev. 4:3]). Where Israel failed, He would now succeed.

Already as a child God had called Him out of Egypt like Israel (cf. Hosea 11:1; Matt. 2:14). Then, like Israel, He passed through the Jordan (in baptism), and now His task was to spend 40 days in the wilderness (a day for a year of Israel's wilderness sojourn), preach for about 1,260 days (a day for a year of Israel's kingdom), and endure about 3.5 days of great tribulation (His trial and death) that Israel was to suffer in years if it did not repent (during the war with Rome between A.D. 66 and 70). By offering Himself as a perfect sacrifice, He aimed to "take away the guilt of the community by making atonement for them before the Lord" (Lev. 10:17, NIV). Both His death and resurrection would be a corporate one—which is how He could apply to Himself a national "we" text, such as Hosea 6:3, which in the LXX reads "in the third day we shall resurrect and live before him." It was Jesus' task, as Israel, to take upon Himself the suffering of the nation. Then when He rose again, His resurrection would be the resurrection of His people to a new life and a new kingdom. It would be a corporate resurrection. When He rose, we rose!

But where is the evidence that Jesus had this day-for-a-year idea in mind? Consider Luke 13:32: "Go ye and tell that fox, Behold, I cast out devils, and I do cures to day and to morrow, and the third day I shall be perfected." This suggests a three-day (i.e., three-year) plan for Jesus' ministry, something we find confirmed by Luke 13:7: "For three years now I've been coming to look for fruit on this fig tree and haven't found any. Cut it down! Why should it use up the soil?" (NIV). The three days of Luke 13:32 correspond to the three years of verse 7.

Still, the evidence is not quite convincing—until we look at Jesus' source for the day-for-a-year idea: Ezekiel. But first we need to demonstrate that the prophet heavily influenced Him. In fact, He modeled His ministry after Ezekiel in several ways:

1. Ezekiel, like Jesus, was called "son of man" (Ezek. 2:1, 3, 6, 8, etc.).
2. Ezekiel, like Jesus, spoke in parables (Ezek. 17:2; 24:3). The Greek word employed in these verses is the term "parable" as used in the Gospels.
3. Ezekiel provides the basis for at least two of Jesus' parables:
   • The parable of the lost sheep (Luke 15:3-7) derives from Ezekiel 34:6, 11-16.
   • The judgment of the sheep and goats (Matt. 25:31-46) echoes Ezekiel 34:17.
4. Ezekiel went only to "the lost sheep of the house of Israel" and not to foreigners (see Ezek. 2:3; 3:4-6). Well, so did Jesus (Matt. 10:6; 15:24; see also Acts 5:31; 10:36; Rom. 15:8). That was His own perception of His mission, at least initially.
5. Ezekiel, like Jesus, was to be a "sign" (*semeion*) for his people (Ezek. 12:11; 24:24; cf. Matt. 24:30; Luke 2:12, 34; 11:30).

So we know Jesus drew many ideas from Ezekiel. All right then, consider yet another parallel, the most important one for understanding the self-concept of Jesus. It provides the rationale that enabled Him to see Himself as a vicarious sin-bearer, including the day-for-a-year idea: "This will be a sign to the people of Israel. Then lie on your left side and *put the sin of the house of Israel upon yourself. You are to bear their sin* for the number of days you lie on your side. I have assigned you *the same number of days as the years of their sin.* So for 390 days you will bear the sin of the people of Israel. After you have finished this, lie down again, this time on your right side, and bear the sin of the people of Judah. *I have assigned you 40 days, a day for each year*" (Ezek. 4:3-6, NIV).

Jesus apparently saw Himself as bearing the guilt of the people, passing over the ground of their failure, this time with success, so that the nation, or at least all who chose Him as their Savior, might escape the coming wrath. But eventually what was happening to Him would also take place among those who did not accept Him (Luke 23:28-31; cf. Ezek. 20:47). Their city, left without a savior, would be besieged and conquered (Ezek. 4:1).

So Jesus set out to recapitulate Israel's 40 years "fasting" in the wilderness.

\* \* \*

Wouldn't it be nice to know what Jesus was thinking about? What passage of Scripture did He spend His time meditating on during the last part of His 40 days in the desert?

Well, the clues are all there; let's figure it out! Every single one of Jesus' answers to the devil comes from Deuteronomy 5-8.

Deuteronomy was one of the most important documents ever written. It contains one of the longest speeches in world history, the farewell speech of Moses—a man who complained that he couldn't speak (Ex. 4:10). It is the second (*deutero*) law (*nomy*), the law restated—with a bit more grace than when first given in Exodus, Leviticus, and Numbers, or so it seems to me. Deuteronomy influenced the Bill of Rights of the United States Constitution: our property rights (ninth and tenth amendments) are from Deuteronomy 19:14; the right to trial by jury (sixth amendment) is from Deuteronomy 19:15; and the right to freedom from unreasonable search and seizure (fourth amendment) is from Deuteronomy 24:10, 11.

According to Joshua Berman, "the book of Deuteronomy has a dual agenda in its blueprint for the polity. First it rejects the exclusionary power strategies exhibited routinely in the monarchic systems of the ancient Near East, instead proposing a collective power strategy, in which power is not only shared, but is primarily invested in the community. Then Deuteronomy rejects the institutions and language of tribal patriarchy in favor of collective, national identity."[2] Deuteronomy brought a new order to the world. The United States of America is a graft from that shoot.

And what portion of Deuteronomy was Jesus thinking about during those final days of His wilderness experience? Well, most likely it was Deuteronomy 5-8—the passage that contains the most important material for any Jewish believer of Jesus' day and also the most pertinent material to His situation at the time. I suggest that these chapters enable us to get inside His mind during His desert struggle.

First, we find the Ten Commandments in Deuteronomy 5:7-21.

This is followed by the Shema (pronounced *shem-AH*) in Deuteronomy 6:4-9, the most sacred passage of the Scriptures for an orthodox Jew. To this day they repeat it daily from memory: "Hear, O Israel: The Lord our God, the Lord is one. Love the Lord your God with all your heart and with all your soul and with all your strength. These commandments that I give you today are to be on your hearts. Impress them on your children. Talk about them when you sit at home and when you walk along the road, when you lie down and when you get up. Tie them as symbols on your hands and bind them on your foreheads. Write them on the doorframes of your houses and on your gates" (NIV).

Notice how much fundamental doctrine the passage contains:

1. The central teaching of Judaism: monotheism.

2. The principle of love that sums up the commandments, cited by Jesus in Matthew 22:37; Mark 12:30, 33; and Luke 10:27; cf. 1 John 5:3.

3. The basis for religious education, which has done great things for God's people. Perhaps that is one reason Jewish scholars and scientists, after millennia of scriptural education, have received nearly one-fourth of all the Nobel Peace Prizes ever awarded, wildly out of proportion to their numbers (the world now has fewer Jews than Seventh-day Adventists).

4. The idea that the commandments are like a sign in the hand and in the forehead, an idea found also in Exodus 13:9, 16 and Deuteronomy 11:18 and which informs the symbolism of Revelation 7:3; 9:4; 13:16; 14:1, 9; 20:4; 22:4.

But the reason Jesus was contemplating this passage, besides its importance is revealed when we have to analyze His answers to the tempter.

According to Luke 4:1, Jesus, full of the Holy Spirit, was led by the Spirit into the wilderness or desert—where for 40 days the devil tempted or tested—Him. He ate nothing during those days, and at the end of them He was naturally hungry.

Some people question whether it is even possible to go for 40 days without eating. Not only is it possible, but it is estimated that about 10,000 Christians in South Korea—one of the most Christian nations on earth—have done it. It is a fast way (pun not intended) to jump to a higher level of spiritual experience, not to mention to lose some weight.

Here is what happens to the body with an extended fast. You feel increasing hunger, of course, until about the third day, after which the body stops burning glucose and the liver starts processing body fat in a process called ketosis. At that point the hunger gradually recedes, and a peaceful feeling of mild euphoria replaces it. Up to a point, fasting is good for us. That's the good news. Three or four weeks later, for most people, the body goes into "starvation mode," and starts mining the muscles and vital organs for energy, and loss of bone marrow becomes life-threatening. The hunger comes back and just keeps growing until one is too weak to do anything about it. Still, it can take 50 to 70 days to die from fasting.

But some have fasted much longer than that.

Paul Hattaway's book *The Heavenly Man* (2002) is the story of "Brother Yun," one of the apostles of modern Christianity in China. The book is an amazing testament of faith, showing how God's miraculous power can transform the most hostile environment. While undergoing torture in 1984 Yun fasted in prison *with no liquids of any kind* for a total of 74 days, which is impossible without a miracle. Hattaway tells the story in detail and names witnesses.

The *Postgraduate Medical Journal* (March 1973, pp. 203-209) tells the fascinating story of one 27-year-old, A. B., who had ample reserves of fat. He successfully completed a 382-day fast, earning him not only a place in the *Guinness Book of World Records,* but also reaching his goal of losing 276 pounds without ill effect.

Maybe you should try a 40-day fast!

The devil no doubt waited until Jesus was famished. Taking advantage of His weakness, he began the temptations where he usually does: on the level of the physical. "If you are the Son of God," he whispered, "tell this stone to become bread" (Luke 4:3, NIV).

"If?" Jesus did not accept doubt wrapped up in an "if." You may recall in Mark 9:22 that at the foot of the mount of transfiguration Jesus met with the father of a demon-possessed boy who said to him "*If you can* do anything, take pity on us and help us" (NIV).

" *'If you can'?*" Jesus said. "Everything is possible for one who believes" (verse 23, NIV).

But Jesus didn't challenge the devil to abandon his doubt. He knew he wouldn't. Instead Jesus merely answers, "It is written: 'Man shall not live on bread alone' " (Luke 4:4).

What was wrong with what the devil asked Jesus to do? Well, it was self-ish. He had come there to depend on God. Now Satan was tempting Him to rely on Himself. "Take matters into Your own hands"—something like what Abraham did. He decided to have children by a servant girl to help God out, because his wife was barren, and the Lord seemed to be dawdling in fulfilling His promise to make him a mighty nation with many descendants.

How did that work out for Abraham? The two nations that descended from Isaac and Ishmael are still at each other's throats to this day in the Near East.

Or take Jacob, who decided to aid God by stealing the birthright blessing from his father, Isaac. And how did that work out?

No, Jesus said, I won't do it. Some things are more important than food.

It is one thing to help God out by going to the store and buying food so that you won't starve, and quite another to use supernatural powers that nobody else has, just for your own benefit. Jesus left it up to God whether to work a miracle or not for Him. He did not ask for miracles merely to aid Himself.

When in 2008 I was seriously ill with mesenteric thrombosis (a blood clot in the bowel) and lost four feet of necrotic colon, I put myself in God's hands and told Him what He did with me was His business. Why should I be spared death when millions more worthy than I had died? Everybody dies. "Have Your way with me, God. Do what You will." That was my actual prayer. At no time did I pray to be healed. I have many serious faults, but this is one lesson I think I have learned. Let God do what He wants, and be at peace. Stop trying to change His mind for your own advantage.

My wife did not feel the same way at all. She was praying for all she was worth that God would keep me alive. My members were praying too, but not with her fervor. The Lord worked miracles—for her sake. I only hope that if my wife were as sick as I was that I would pray for her with all the fervor that she did for me. It is not a sin to pray for a miracle for ourselves, but it may imply some spiritual immaturity. Mature Christians ask for miracles for others, like my wife did for me.

If she were sick, I'm pretty sure she wouldn't pray to be saved from death. She has always made it very clear to me that she does not want to live without me, and most definitely plans to be the first to die. I can't seem to talk her out of that.

But God has His own plans. His will is best. The things we think we need are not what we must have at all. But the things we most require, we can't see, so we don't even know about them. Yet most of our concern goes toward things we can see but don't have.

Jesus taught us to pray for our basic needs. "Give us this day our daily bread" (Matt. 6:11). Remember that He presented this prayer to a group of men who had given up their jobs, so such a concern was very real to them. "You worry about fishing for men, and then God will take care of your needs."

What did Jesus mean that we do not live by bread alone? Babies abandoned by their mothers can receive all the physical nourishment they need in a warm box in the hospital, but if no one picks them up and holds and coddles and loves them, they will fail to thrive. Most will die. Why? Because food is not enough.

That reminds me of the title of a James Bond film: *The World Is Not Enough*. If I had just one sermon to preach, that might be the title. The whole world, with all its wonders, temptations, beauties, and pleasures, is not enough. Sometimes we get bogged down in its enticing diversions, but what we really want is God. He can make a million worlds. One world is never enough, but God alone is always more than enough. We cannot live by bread alone.

Job once said, "I have not departed from the commands of his lips; I have treasured the words of his mouth more than my daily bread" (Job 23:12, NIV). God's Word is our bread and butter—it brings fatness of the soul.

Jesus, after His encounter with the Samaritan woman at the well, told His disciples, "I have food to eat that you know nothing about" (John 4:32, NIV). Those who live to bless others, to give them the bread of life, know exactly what He meant. That's the spiritual vitamins that kept Jesus going. Food like that nourishes our souls. God grant that we might start thinking more about invisible food.

But now let's analyze Jesus' answer in the context of His source. Why did He choose this particular reply, keeping in mind all we have learned so far about what He thought He was doing in the desert? "Remember how the Lord your God led you all the way in the wilderness these forty years, to humble and test you in order to know what was in your heart, whether or not you would keep his commands. He humbled you, causing you to hunger and then feeding you with manna, which neither you nor your ancestors had known, to teach you that man does not live on bread alone but on every word that comes from the mouth of the Lord" (Deut. 8:2, 3, NIV).

Can you see why the passage would be especially significant for Jesus at this time? If not, read it again.

During those 40 days Jesus was recapitulating the 40-year experience of Israel in the desert. For all we know, He might have hoped that God would send manna, but the Lord *didn't*! Yet Jesus would accept whatever the Father wanted to give Him. He would hunger until God wanted to feed Him. Jesus would not cheat and short-circuit it.

Notice one more thing. Two verses later the passage in Deuteronomy reads: "Know then in your heart that as a man disciplines his son, so the Lord your God disciplines you" (Deut. 8:5). How precious this passage must have been to Jesus while He was in the desert. God was disciplining His Son. Let the discipline work. It was all in the loving purpose of the tender heart of His Father. Anything is bearable if one knows that an all-knowing, all-caring Father is in control and is calibrating and controlling the outcome.

After all, Jesus wasn't here just for Himself—He was forging a new future for His people, those to be incorporated in the new Israel. He was building His kingdom. But before He could rule over others, He had to be able to rule over Himself, His passions, His appetites. Here is another one of life's great truths: If you can win the hardest battle of all—the battle with self—then no foe can stand against you. You must, in the strength that God provides, first conquer yourself. Then you can defeat anything.

So if God wanted Jesus hungry, He would hunger. And we, the servants, are not above our Master. If God allows tribulation to come to us, then let's tribulate! And thank Him for the privilege of sharing in His sufferings.

Because it's not about us. Millions of invisible eyes may be watching us, and invisible majesties in the heavenly realms. Our suffering may purify us, but that is not all that is going on. Something bigger than we can now understand is happening, and we are playing our incomprehensible yet crucial roles in the great drama of the ages that will reconcile all created things to their Creator.

\* \* \*

Now, the devil is a fast learner. Jesus had quoted Scripture. So Satan thought, *OK, I can do that too. I'll fight him on his own battleground.*

"The devil led him up to a high place and showed him in an instant all the kingdoms of the world. And he said to him, 'I will give you all their authority and splendor; it has been given to me, and I can give it to anyone I want to.

So if you worship me, it will all be yours' " (Luke 4:5-7, NIV).

Why does Luke switch the order of the temptations here from the one in Matthew? Nobody knows. Jerome Murphy O'Connor has pointed out that, in Matthew, the three tests take place at progressively higher altitudes. For the first test Jesus is "led up" from the Jordan River "into the desert." He then rises to the crest on which Jerusalem, the site of the second test, rests. Finally, the story concludes on an "exceeding high mountain" (Matt. 4:8). Luke for some reason breaks this beautiful pattern.

But Luke adds something very interesting to the story that Matthew missed.

The next temptation brings us right back into Daniel 7 again. Commentators don't seem to notice this, but the devil is alluding to Scripture again. His offer to give Jesus authority over all the kingdoms of the world is an echo of Daniel 7:14: "He was given authority, glory and sovereign power; all nations and peoples of every language worshiped him" (NIV).

Daniel 7:13, 14 formed Jesus' identity and is the most important passage in the Old Testament for understanding who He thought He was. It gave Him His favorite title, His kingdom, His coming, and His right to authority, glory, worship, and dominion. Jesus cites it more than any other passage. The passage was as foundational to Christianity as Daniel 8:14 is to Adventism.

But there's more. Satan's claim to bestow those kingdoms on anyone he wished is an allusion to Daniel 4:17, 32, which reserves the prerogative to God alone. Daniel 4 is the story of the humbling of Nebuchadnezzar, when God took away his reason for seven years.

"The decision is announced by messengers, the holy ones declare the verdict, so that the living may know that the Most High is sovereign over all kingdoms on earth and *gives them to anyone he wishes* and sets over them the lowliest of people. . . . Seven times will pass by for you until you acknowledge that the Most High is sovereign over all kingdoms on earth and *gives them to anyone he wishes*" (Dan. 4:17-32, NIV).

Now compare the passage with what the devil said to Jesus: "I will give you all their authority and splendor; it has been given to me, and *I can give it to anyone I want to.*"

What is the devil doing here? He seems to be pretending to be an angelic messenger of God, a "holy one," sent from the Lord to offer Jesus a seductively simple shortcut to the glorious destiny of world domination that He knew had to come through suffering. He is evidently hoping that Jesus, in His weakness, will buy the deception.

It is likely that the devil came to Jesus in garments of dazzling light. Perhaps Paul alludes to this event when he says that "Satan himself masquerades as an angel of light" (2 Cor. 11:14, NIV). Here in the desert a shining angel claims that he represents God, who gives the kingdom to anyone He wants to. All Jesus has to do is to worship him, and in so doing would He not just be worshiping God?

Luke 4:8 reports that Jesus answered, "It is written: 'Worship the Lord your God and serve him only' " (NIV). That's a quote from Deuteronomy 6:13: "Fear the Lord your God, serve him only and take your oaths in his name" (NIV).

Curses! Foiled again! *Well,* Satan said to himself, *maybe one more scripture before I give up.* So he takes Jesus to the highest point of the Temple in Jerusalem and says, "Throw Yourself down. After all, don't You believe God's promise that He will command His angels to guard You and lift You up so that You won't strike Your foot against a stone?"

Jesus answered, "It is said: 'Do not put the Lord your God to the test' " (see Luke 4:9-12). He is quoting Deuteronomy 6:16: "Do not put the Lord your God to the test as you did at Massah" (NIV). Jesus managed to answer all of Satan's temptations without venturing outside the space of two chapters in Deuteronomy (6 and 8).

It is not wise to create a situation in which God has to work a miracle to save us. That's not faith; it's presumption—unless we are on the battlefield for Christ and feel called to take a risk to advance His cause when we cannot fully see the way. That's different. But just doing a trick to see if God will save us does not qualify. That puts us on the level of snake-handlers.

God is not a mouse in our laboratory that we can experiment with. He is the Experimenter, and we are the subjects. Testing Him is above our pay grade. Rather, it is the superior that tests the inferior. "We should not test Christ" (1 Cor. 10:9, NIV).

There is one exception, though, in which God does ask us to put Him to the test: " 'Bring the whole tithe into the storehouse, that there may be food in my house. Test me in this,' says the Lord Almighty, 'and see if I will not throw open the floodgates of heaven and pour out so much blessing that there will not be room enough to store it' " (Mal. 3:10, NIV). Other than that, if we want to test anyone, we should test ourselves, examine our own ways (Lam. 3:40; 2 Cor. 13:5).

Luke 4:13 tells us that "when the devil had finished all this tempting, he left him until an opportune time" (NIV). The devil comes to us at opportune times: when we are tired and weak, when we are hungry, or when we are exhausted. Those are the occasions when he's there to tempt. And those are the dangerous times. Right after we've been on top of the mountain, on a spiritual high, then in the emotional exhaustion that follows we are prone to discouragement and spiritual weakness.

There in the desert, battling snakes and scorpions, Jesus recapitulated the history of Israel—one day of fasting for every year of Israel's desert sojourn. Israel had encountered the same hazards during the 40 years God led them through the desert, "that thirsty and waterless land, with its venomous snakes and scorpions" (Deut. 8:15, NIV). Notice that passage is also from Deuteronomy 5-8. Jesus conquered the snakes and scorpions there in the desert. That's how He could tell His disciples, "I have given you authority to trample on snakes and scorpions and to overcome all the power of the enemy; nothing will harm you" (Luke 10:19, NIV).

Jesus came out of the desert having spent 40 days alone with nothing but God. There His faith grew strong as His mission took shape. He learned how little it took to get by. Abandoning possessions frees the soul. Nothing but God, it turns out, is more than enough.

Then Jesus went back to civilization with a new gleam in His eye, a new fire in His heart, and a laser focus on the one thing that mattered: the soon-coming kingdom. Only now He not only had a mission but also a strategy not unlike that of the contemporary cynic philosophers: simplify, simplify, simplify. Get rid of every encumbrance. Focus on one thing. With a new courage and authority, He asked others to follow in His footsteps and abandon everything to preach the kingdom.

Shortly after Jesus' return, according to Mark 1, Herod had John the Baptist imprisoned, so Jesus stepped into the leadership vacuum. He gathered a group of disciples and cut away their ties to conventional culture. They listened as He taught, and watched as He healed. After a period of training He sent them out to share what they had learned.

But He did something really crazy. Jesus dispatched them without jobs or provisions.

How then were they to support themselves? His answer was: "Do not worry, saying, 'What shall we eat?' or 'What shall we drink?' or 'What shall we wear?' " (Matt 6:31, NIV; cf. Luke 12:22). Stay with the locals, and eat whatever they offer you (Luke 10:7, 8). The disciples would find themselves forced to rely on that part of their Lord's Prayer that well-salaried Christians today find merely puzzling: "Give us this day our daily bread" (Matt 6:11; cf. Luke 11:3).

And God did provide. When the 70 disciples returned from their unprovisioned missionary journey, Jesus asked them whether they had lacked anything. "Nothing," they replied (Luke 22:35).

That is remarkable, as Jesus had forbidden the disciples to carry luggage, money, or supplies (Luke 9:3; 10:4; 22:35), thus outdoing even the local Cynics, who at least allowed a little luggage (the wallet, a sort of knapsack) and a staff.

Imagine a modern evangelist traveling without luggage, wallet, cash, credit cards, cell phone, or a change of clothes.

But Jesus had a hidden agenda: The disciples' apparent helplessness maximized contact with others. It made them vulnerable instead of self-sufficient, dependent instead of independent, enabling them to make friends and touch hearts with their witness. People who don't need people don't change people. Moreover, it drove them to prayer. The disciples would have to rely on God. What better way to strengthen the muscle of faith?

Jesus was, after all, only asking them to do what He had already done. Surely, if He could survive with nothing in the desert, they could do the same in the villages.

And so the disciples learned that *"nothing but God"* is more than enough. The Lord alone is sufficient.

Have you learned that truth? It can bring great peace. But you may not believe it. Many don't. Here is one simple test to show you whether you do or not. Are you tithing? If not, then you don't believe. You don't think God can take care of you.

That's just a little test, a trivial one. The disciples gave up 100 percent of their money to the cause of Jesus, as we will discover later. Ten percent is the bare minimum—it's where we should start, not the ultimate goal. If we cannot give up a mere 10 percent, with a promise like that found in Malachi 3, then something is terribly wrong. We don't think God is enough.

And if that is the case, well, then, for us, He never will be enough. If we cannot trust Him with 10 percent of our income, then how can we rely on Him with 100 percent of our lives?

Think about it. Trust Him now. Because He wants to be more than enough for you.

---

1. Geza Vermes, *Jesus the Jew: A Historian's Reading of the Gospels* (Philadelphia: Fortress Press, 1981), p. 172.

2. Joshua Berman, "Constitution, Class, and the Book of Deuteronomy," in *Hebraic Political Studies* 1, no. 5 (2006): 523-548.

# CHAPTER 3

# Who Is Jesus?

One thing even an impartial skeptic must admit: Jesus is the most important person of all time. Forget for a moment what the Scriptures say. Just consider objectively the extra-canonical evidence.

People have written more books about Jesus than anyone else who ever lived. In the past 2,000 years millions of books in all languages have at least mentioned His name, and 200,000 to 400,000 books in English since the beginning of print have taken Him as their chief subject. The Library of Congress holds nearly twice as many books on Jesus as the next most discussed individual (Shakespeare).

Not only has Jesus been the subject of more books, He has been the theme of more songs. We sing about people important to us. Imagine a catalogue of all songs broadcast in all languages worldwide in the twenty-first century on every radio and television channel. If we tallied the names of every historical human being mentioned in the lyrics, Jesus would win hands down. I cannot even imagine who the runner-up might be.

But that's a hypothetical experiment. Here's a real one: Computer scientists Steven Skiena and Charles Ward devised a mathematical algorithm for categorizing famous people through quantitative analysis. They found that Jesus is the most significant person of all time. Their algorithm, using *Wikipedia,* ranks individuals just as Google does Web pages: by aggregating the traces of millions of opinions. "If all roads lead to Rome, Rome must be a pretty important place."[1] The names after Jesus are (2) Napoleon; (3) Muhammad; (4) Shakespeare; (5) Lincoln; (6) Washington; (7) Hitler; (8) Aristotle; (9) Alexander the Great. Barack Obama came in at 111.

For obvious reasons, Skiena and Ward did not include Santa Claus, one of the most beloved figures around the world. But Santa Claus is, of course, Saint Nicholas (A.D. 270-343), Bishop of Myra, a devout follower of Jesus Christ who dedicated his life to giving away his inherited wealth to help the poor. Without Jesus there would have been no Santa Claus.

And speaking of *Wikipedia,* Jesus is one of the most edited, contested, defended, elaborated, and linked-to entries, with hundreds of footnotes. Someone is writing a book on the colorful history of that *Wikipedia* entry itself.

*The Jesus Film* (1979) is far and away the most influential movie ever made, having been dubbed into more than 1,200 languages and seen by well more than half of the world's population because of the work of missionary organizations. By way of comparison, *The Passion of the Christ* (2004), grossing more than $600 million so far, is subtitled (not dubbed) in only 38 languages. Available in full on the Internet, *The Jesus Film* has produced more than 200 million decisions for Christ.

Jesus' influence extends even into space. Although NASA did not publicize it, the first beverage ever poured on the moon and the first food eaten there were the elements of the Christian Communion service (by Buzz Aldrin on July 20, 1969).

And then there is the fact that we number our years from His birth. The apogee of humanity, He split time in two. The history of civilization is Jesus versus everything else, and that will continue for a very long time.

So why is this 2,000-year-old so popular? "Time has not faded the vividness of his image," wrote Solomon B. Freehof, a rabbi and an unbeliever. "Poetry still sings his praise. He is still the living comrade of countless lives. No Moslem ever sings, 'Mohammed, lover of my soul,' nor does any Jew say of Moses, the teacher, 'I need thee every hour.' "[2]

Quite apart from the question of whether He was God in the flesh, Jesus is one of the most fascinating figures of history. A self-sacrificing teacher of subversive wisdom, His spiritual legacy has arguably done more to empower the powerless than all other revolutionaries who ever lived. He is still the single most influential architect of the future of our planet, if only because one-third of the human race claims Him as Lord.

Notice that I have not so far relied on any article of faith, but only empirical data. That evidence alone tells us that Jesus is the world's most important person.

The twenty-first century is still obsessed with Jesus. He is as controversial now as He was when He walked the earth. While the names of other religious icons arouse little reaction in polite Western society, His name, spoken with respect, still produces electricity. Even the contemporary use of His name as a swearword offers evidence of its power. People choose swearwords because of their power to evoke emotion. Strangely, no other name of any historical human is so widely used as an oath. Lapsed Jews do not profane the name of

Moses, nor former Muslims that of Muhammad. Buddhists and Hindus curse, not by using the name of Buddha or Brahma or Krishna, but that of Jesus.

Curious, isn't it? What's so special about the name of Jesus?

\* \* \*

One undiscovered truth about Jesus that may shock some people is the origin of the term "Messiah," another name used to refer to Jesus. The Jews of Jesus' day were expecting a military conqueror to deliver them. Why? Because the Hebrew scriptures always portray the *Messiach,* or Anointed One, as a military conqueror. Let's start with the Torah—the five books of Moses.

Balaam's Messianic prophecy in Numbers 24:17-19 speaks of the "Star out of Jacob" who would crush his enemies, including Moab, Edom, and Seir. In Deuteronomy 18:15 Moses predicts that God would send Israel "a Prophet . . . like unto me." And what sort of prophet was Moses? He was a military conqueror who, according to Josephus,[3] commanded the armies of Egypt in victory against the Ethiopians before he led the armies of Israel in victory over the Canaanites.

The psalms depict the Messiah as a military conqueror as well. The most-often-cited psalm in the New Testament is Psalm 110, the whole point of which is the promise of military victory to the Messianic king of Israel. The second-most-often-cited one is Psalm 118, which says of the Messiah: "All the nations surrounded me, but in the name of the Lord I cut them down" (verse 10, NIV). Again, Psalm 2 declares that the "anointed" (verse 2) "king" in Jerusalem (verse 6) will dash the nations in pieces (verse 9), and Acts 4:25-27 and Revelation 2:27; 12:5; 19:15 applies the prophecy to Jesus. Later Jewish expectations associated both Psalm 2 and 118 with the eschatological war with Gog and Magog (Ezek. 38, 39; Rev. 20:7-10).

In the psalms God's covenant promise to the Messianic "Son of David" was that "*the enemy will not get the better of him; the wicked will not oppress him. I will crush his foes before him and strike down his adversaries*" (Pss. 89:22, 23; cf. 125:3; 2 Kings 17:39; Isa. 14:2; 52:1, 2; 54:14; Jer. 30:8; Zech. 9:8). By Jesus' time Jews understood it to mean that the Messiah would make an end of paying tribute to Rome. Hence the Jewish tax revolt of A.D. 6.

What about the prophets? One well-known Messianic passage is Isaiah 9:6: "Unto us a child is born . . ." Military victory is an obvious part of the picture: "The rod of his oppressor, you have broken as on the day of Midian. For every boot of the tramping warrior in battle tumult and every garment rolled in blood will be burned as fuel for the fire" (verses 4, 5, ESV).

Isaiah 11, another Messianic passage, describes the coming scion of Jesse (verses 1, 10). He first appears as a Spirit-anointed judge of the poor and meek (verses 2-4), and then, in the same breath, as a conqueror who "shall smite the earth: with the rod of his mouth, and with the breath of his lips shall he slay the wicked" (verse 4). Under his leadership Israel would "swoop down on the slopes of Philistia to the west; together they will plunder the people to the east. They will subdue Edom and Moab, and the Ammonites will be subject to them" (verse 14, NIV).

It is because *messiach* connotes a military conqueror that Isaiah 45:1 can apply the term to Cyrus.

Isaiah 53 lacks the term *messiach,* so the passage does not contradict the assertion that the Messiah is always a military conqueror. We will discuss it elsewhere.

Micah's Messianic prophecy about the coming Ruler to be born in Bethlehem "whose origins are from of old" (Micah 5:2, NIV) also notes that the "Daughter of Zion" would "break to pieces many nations" (Micah 4:13, NIV). "The remnant of Jacob will be among the nations . . . like a young lion among flocks of sheep, which mauls and mangles as it goes, and no one can rescue" (Micah 5:8). In Daniel 2 the kingdom of God will "crush all those kingdoms and bring them to an end" (verse 44, NIV).

Zion's humble king "riding on a donkey" (Zech. 9:9, NIV) will bring peace to the earth by leading Israel in battle against her enemies (verse 13), and "the Lord Almighty will shield them. They will destroy and overcome with slingstones" (verse 15, NIV). "On that day I will make the clans of Judah like a firepot in a woodpile, like a flaming torch among sheaves. They will consume all the surrounding peoples right and left, but Jerusalem will remain intact in her place" (Zech. 12:6, NIV). The remnant of Israel would wield their swords in holy war against the nations (Ps. 149:2-9; see also Deut. 7:16; 20:10-18; Pss. 58:10; 106:34).

This idea of a conquering Messiah who delivers the faithful from their persecutors flows from the prophets right into the New Testament in passages such as Luke 1:67-74, 2 Thessalonians 1:5-10, and Revelation 17:14 and 19:15, 19. In fact, we still believe in a conquering Messiah today. That is what is going to happen at the Second Coming. And if the Jewish leaders had accepted Jesus, the "come with power" aspect of the program, involving the overthrow of the nations, might have happened much sooner.

But we find still another tradition in the Old Testament. In the original struggle to conquer Palestine God intended to do all the fighting for His people (Ex. 14:13, 14; 23:23; Deut. 1:30; Joshua 24:12; 2 Kings 19:35; 2 Chron. 20:15, 17).

I suspect that Jesus may have understood Isaiah 63:1-6 to mean that the Lord would tread down the nations alone, without the help of the people. Hosea 1:7 promises: "I will show love to Judah; and I will save them—not by bow, sword or battle, or by horses and horsemen, but I, the Lord their God" (NIV).

By the time of Daniel it was apparent that Israel's oppressors must be destroyed "without hands" (Dan. 2:34, 45; see Dan. 8:25; 11:45). God would do the fighting.

The Targums were the popular *Clear Word* or *Living Bible* of Jesus' day— interpretative paraphrases of the Scriptures with added commentary right in the text. Jesus no doubt shared the opinion expressed in the Targum on Song of Solomon 8:4: "King Messiah will say, 'I adjure you, my people, House of Israel. Why are you warring against the nations of the earth to leave the Exile? Why are you rebelling against the forces of Gog and Magog? Wait a little longer until the nations who come up to make war against Jerusalem are destroyed, and after that the Lord of the World will remember for you the love of the righteous, and let it be His will to redeem you.' "

So Jesus had nothing to say about the overthrow of Rome. In His day all talk of war was dangerous, not only to the speaker but to the entire Jewish nation. Besides, Israel's deliverance would depend more on its spiritual progress than its physical strength. Jesus' first concern was to secure the repentance and allegiance of His own people. God would take care of the Romans.

In the New Testament the forces of heaven do all the fighting in the final battle that will destroy every government on earth at the Second Coming (cf. Rev. 6:15; 16:14; 19:19). In the Apocalypse the glorified Jesus wields the sword of justice (see Rev. 1:16; 2:12, 16; 13:10; 19:15, 21).

But while He was on earth He told His followers to put away their swords, turn the other cheek, and bless their persecutors (Matt. 5:38-48; 26:52). Only in the sense that His message would provoke fierce opposition and divide families did Jesus say, "I did not come to bring peace, but a sword" (Matt. 10:34).

In contrast, we find the believers themselves commanded to slay the infidels in the scriptures of both Judaism (Deut. 7:16; 20:10-18; 1 Kings 8:44; Pss. 58:10; 106:34; 149:6-9; etc.) and Islam (e.g., Sura 2:216; 9:5, 19-21, 40; 48:28; etc.). Both Moses and Muhammad were militant warlords whose forces killed thousands of people in their lifetimes. Their followers preyed on their enemies, while Jesus' followers prayed *for* their enemies (Rom. 12:14, 20, 21; 1 Cor. 4:12, 13; 1 Peter 2:21-23). The Christian's only weapons were to be spiritual (Eph. 6:12-17; 2 Cor. 10:4)—later aberrations to the contrary notwithstanding.

\* \* \*

During His lifetime Jesus did not prefer the term "Messiah" (Hebrew) or Christ (Greek). Instead His desired self-designation was "Son of man." Let's look at the significance of that title.

As we have already noted, it has always been thought to come from Daniel 7. That is quite obvious. However, in the last half of the twentieth century this became the subject of extensive debate. Some scholars argued that the term is merely a synonym for "I" or "me." We see that clearly is the case in Mark 8:27 and Matthew 16:13, Matthew 5:11 and Luke 6:22, and Matthew 10:32 and Luke 12:8, in which one passage has a personal pronoun while the parallel one reads "the Son of man." The Aramaic language has a precedent for such a usage. Jesus appears to be using a self-depreciating term that indicated the speaker as a typical man, or as one of a class, that is, "one such as I," "a man like me." Scholars such as Barnabas Linders, Maurice Casey, Geza Vermes, and others have argued variations on such a theme.

The existence of the Aramaic idiom, however, does not explain the facts. First of all, one can maintain such an idea only by distinguishing the "authentic" sayings from the "inauthentic" ones that contradict the new interpretation. Of course, one can prove anything this way.

Secondly, the "Son of man" sayings on the lips of Jesus are self-aggrandizing, not self-denigrating. Even the few that at first glance appear to be exceptions, "The Son of Man has no place to lay his head" (Luke 9:58, NIV) and "The Son of Man did not come to be served, but to serve" (Matt. 20:28, NIV), only highlight the irony that so exalted a figure as the Son of man would assume such a lowly role. It is a self-reference, yes, but one with an agenda. When occasionally identified as "the Christ" (Mark 8:29-31; 14:61, 62), Jesus responds by speaking of what "the Son of man" will do, wishing, evidently, to replace the concept of "Messiah," which carried overtones of revolt and sedition ever since the uprisings after the death of Herod the Great, with the more modest and ambiguous "Son of man," a term that, however, is at the same time an allusion to the glorious being of Daniel 7. Jesus has found a way of assuming a Messianic pose without making explicit claims. On His lips, then, "Son of man" is a double entendre, both self-denigrating (as far as the authorities might be concerned) and self-exalting (to those who are in on the allusion) at the same time!

To claim that "Son of Man" emphasizes the humanity of Jesus, while "Son of God" His divinity, is to miss the point. "Son of Man" is actually the more exalted title. The Roman emperor was officially honored in 27 B.C. with the title Imperator Caesar Augustus Divi Filius (son of god). So calling Himself "Son of God" would have been dangerous for Jesus. But the "Son of Man" reigns over all rulers everywhere (Dan 7:14). Thus Jesus is above Caesar. It was a clever way to assert His status in a manner the Romans wouldn't quite understand. It was a clever way to assert His status in a manner the Romans wouldn't quite understand.

The "Son of Man" is the title of an exalted, Messianic figure in the "Similitudes" (1 Enoch 37-71). Well known at the time, 1 Enoch was the book that influenced the New Testament more than any other non-canonical writing. We simply don't know whether this section of Enoch—the Similitudes—was written slightly earlier or slightly later than the time of Jesus. If later, Jesus may have participated in forming the tradition. But if earlier, then He was employing an idea already familiar within a certain strand of Judaism. The bottom line is that "Son of man" is a Messianic title of exalted significance.

* * *

Was Jesus omniscient? Did He know everything? The disciples exclaim to Jesus that He knows "all things" in John 16:30 and 21:17. But "all things" is a relative phrase. The Samaritan woman at the well said that Jesus told her "all things" that she ever did (John 4:29, 39), and Jesus promised that the Comforter would teach the disciples "all things" (John 14:26). John claims his readers know "all things" in 1 John 2:20, 27.

The Gospels indicate that Jesus did indeed have supernatural powers of perception or revelation (Mark 2:8; 14:12-16; Matt. 12:25; 16:8; Luke 6:8; 9:47; John 1:48; 2:25; 4:16-19; 6:64; 16:30; etc.). Some other prophets had similar powers (e.g., 2 Kings 6:12).

But the Gospels also indicate that Jesus did not know some things. The decisive passage is Mark 13:32: "But about that day or hour no one knows, not even the angels in heaven, nor the Son, but only the Father" (NIV). If there was even one thing He didn't know, then there may have been many. While Mark 13:32 is decisive, see also Mark 5:9, 30-32; 6:38; 8:5; and 10:36, in which Jesus has to ask for information.

The New Testament says that Jesus "increased in wisdom" (Luke 2:52), and "learned obedience from what he suffered" (Heb. 5:8, NIV). The evidence suggests that the earthly Jesus was no more omniscient than He was omnipresent, immortal, or unsleeping. He had to learn in the school of hard knocks like any real human being.

Sometimes, in fact, Jesus may have made small mistakes in citing the Old

Testament, as no one back then had Bibles in their bedrooms. Either Jesus or His biographers confused different historical figures.

First, in Mark 2:26 Jesus said: "In the days of Abiathar the high priest, he [David] entered the house of God and ate the consecrated bread, which is lawful only for priests to eat" (NIV). But that actually happened in the days of Ahimelech (1 Sam. 21:1-6). Conservative scholar Daniel B. Wallace provides a thorough analysis of possible solutions in "Mark 2:26 and the Problem of Abiathar" (available online).

But none of these solutions help us solve the second problem: In Matthew 23:35 Jesus made the Jews responsible for all the blood shed from Abel to "Zechariah son of Berekiah" (NIV)—that is, from the first martyr to the last, from Abel in Genesis to Zechariah in Chronicles, the last book in the Hebrew canon. However, the Zechariah in question was not the son of Berekiah (Zech. 1:1, 7), but of Jehoiada (2 Chron. 24:20, 21). Such confusion was widespread.[4]

Two similar misstatements in two different contexts make it difficult to assign the blame to anything other than a momentary lapse on Jesus' part. What do we gain by assigning the problem to the inspired Gospel writers?

Add to this two further Gospel examples of mistaken attribution: Matthew 27:9, 10 cites Zechariah 11:13 but ascribes it incorrectly to Jeremiah, and Mark 1:2 cites Malachi 3:1 but says it came from Isaiah. Now we have four similar errors to explain away, and Occam's razor applies with double force: The simplest explanation is the best.

Neither the Gospel writers nor Jesus had the Scriptures at their fingertips to check references on the spur of the moment. Evidently inspiration does not prevent slips of memory.

The idea that if Jesus was divine then He could not err in any way is no more logical than the belief that He never got hungry or sleepy. Momentary lapses are an innocent human weakness. And the rationalization "false in one, false in all" is not how things work in the real world. In high school my math textbook had answers in the back to some of the exercises. Occasionally one of them was clearly incorrect, by consensus of the class and the teacher, but we did not assume "false in one, false in all" and lose faith in the formulas in the rest of the book.

Yes, but isn't Scripture inspired? Of course. All Scripture, according to 2 Timothy 3:16, is "God-breathed" (NIV). Why, then, these marks of humanity? Scripture may not meet modern ideals of grammatical perfection—for example, "Jerusalem" is consistently spelled one way in John and another in Revelation—yet with all its frailties, Scripture in the hands of a believing and faithful witness is imbued with an inexplicable, life-changing power that no human psychology can match. The whole is greater than the sum of its parts. Just as even a frayed wire still conducts electricity, if plugged in, so God inspires imperfect human beings to write words that somehow convey His glory to those whose hearts are tuned to the frequency of faith. But we have this treasure in earthen vessels, which is why Scripture is imperfect. *We should not expect perfection in an epistle any more than we do in an apostle.* If God can empower imperfect human beings, then He can do the same for imperfect texts.

* * *

Here's another widely debated question about Jesus: Did He have a sinful nature (like Adam after the Fall) or a sinless one (like Adam before the Fall)? The answer to this question, it seems to me, is not entirely clear.

Those who have strong opinions on this question, based on Ellen G. White quotations, should read the more-or-less exhaustive collection of Ellen G. White statements on the issue in the appendix of Woodrow Whidden II's 1997 *Ellen White on the Humanity of Christ.* The book contains an appendix that lists all passages cited by all parties from both sides, arranged chronologically. You may be surprised to find that the matter is considerably less clear than you had thought. You may have never seen some of the strongest statements on the other side.

The same thing is true of the Bible's position on the subject. When you look at all of the relevant passages, it seems that the writers of Scripture were not addressing the same questions we are asking. I regard the question of the exact human nature of Christ as unsolved, and I think arguing about it is not a good thing, because if it were absolutely essential to hold one view or another, God would have made it plainer to us. It is an issue that divides. Let's think about it some more.

But there is one thing we can be certain of. Jesus said, "All power is given unto me in heaven and in earth" (Matt. 28:18). How do we know He was telling the truth? Well, let me tell you a story.

In July 2011 Carol, my wife of 31 years, shared a story she had never told me before. We went out for some ice cream, and as she was reminiscing she remembered something that happened about 1965 or 1966, when she was 13 or 14 years old. The story electrified me, and I grilled her on the details and checked out the address on the Internet.

At the time she lived at 824 Chipley Street, in Westwego, Louisiana, a suburb of New Orleans. She had been invited to a party at the nearby house of a friend on 4th Street, who was one of her classmates at Vic A. Pitre Elementary School.

Eventually the girls started playing with a Ouija board. They asked it questions about the future—but they kept the questions secret and asked them silently so that no one could make up answers. What is my favorite dance band? Will I get married? How many children will I have? With the fingers of the whole group lightly touching the planchette, it would propel itself over the letters and quickly spell out an answer. The girls *ooh*ed and *aah*ed.

At first Carol didn't want to have anything to do with it. Recently baptized, she had been warned against Ouija boards.

"Carol, you do it!" they cried. When she demurred, they persisted. *Lord,* she prayed silently, *I don't know what to do. Please help me.*

Now God has, I believe, a soft spot in His heart for newly baptized young believers who cling to Him. And all the powers of hell are no match for a little girl with God.

Suddenly an idea popped into her head. "OK," she said out loud. "But I won't tell you what I'm going to ask it in advance."

Pausing, she concentrated. Suddenly the planchette moved rapidly across the board, startling her. "Jesus," it spelled. Then it stopped moving.

The Ouija would no longer work.

"Carol, what did you do to it?" the others whined. "What did you ask it?"

"First," she replied, "I asked it who is King of kings and Lord of lords. Then I asked it, 'And who do you serve?' and it wouldn't answer."

The girls tried more questions, with no response. "Carol, you broke it!" they exclaimed. Since they were upset at her for stopping the fun, and she was growing increasingly uneasy about being in the room with the device, she called her mother for a ride home.

Curious, isn't it? What's so special about the name of Jesus?

If Jesus is indeed King of kings and Lord of lords, high and exalted, forever blessed, how could He at the same time be the one who came to die an ugly death on a cross for me? Now that's a mystery! Something to think about for a few thousand years. The answer lies deeper than the intellect. It transcends mere facts and data. Perhaps music can help. Try basking in the beauty of the Brooklyn Tabernacle Choir song "Bless Your Name Forevermore" on YouTube.

---

1. Steven Skiena and Charles B. Word, *Who's Bigger? Where Historical Figures Really Rank*

(New York: Cambridge University Press, 2014), p. 21.

2. Solomon B. Freehof, *Stormers of Heaven* (New York: Harper and Brothers, 1931), p. 210.

3. Josephus, *Antiquities of the Jews* 2.

4. See the discussion in S. A. Blank, "The Death of Zechariah in Rabbinic Literature," *Hebrew Union College Annual* 12/13 (1937-1938): 327-346.

# CHAPTER 4

# The Disciplines of a Disciple

When I was young my family lived by a creek. It had a small waterfall where the water flowed over the roots of a huge eucalyptus tree and fell into a cavern beneath the roots. I loved to be down there where the water just never stopped flowing.

Now that I am older I enjoy visiting waterfalls and looking at pictures of the great ones around the world, such as Victoria, Iguazú, and Niagara. (I've been to two of them.) I love them because to me they are metaphors of God's love and grace that pours down ceaselessly upon us.

Nothing is more important in a disciple of Jesus Christ than love. Would you like to understand the love of God in a deeper way? Here is how you can feel the thunder of God's Niagara of love falling all around you and over you. It's very simple. Not easy, but simple.

Simple and easy are not the same thing. Taking an automobile engine apart and putting it together again is easy if you have lots of experience, but it's not simple. On the other hand, rolling a large rock up a hill is simple but not easy. Trying to draw a perfect circle freehand is simple but not easy. And running 10 miles is also simple but not easy.

Well, here is a simple-but-not-easy exercise for getting a deep knowledge of the love of God. Jesus revealed it in a sermon He preached one day to a group of people sitting on a hillside who were looking every which way to get out from under the great Satan of Rome. "But to you who are listening I say: Love your enemies, do good to those who hate you, bless those who curse you, pray for those who mistreat you. If someone slaps you on one cheek, turn to them the other also. If someone takes your coat, do not withhold your shirt from them. Give to everyone who asks you, and if anyone takes what belongs to you, do not demand it back. Do to others as you would have them do to you" (Luke 6:27-31, NIV).

Disciples have disciplines, and they take the form of spiritual calisthenics.

We know that exercise is good for us. We believe in it, but we don't do it. Although we know the theory, we'd still rather ride when we could walk.

Jeff Bezos, CEO of Amazon, bought a new building for his headquarters years ago. He made himself a promise that he would always use the stairs, never the elevator.

One day when nobody else was working he had to come in to the office. But he had the flu and felt terrible. Although sorely tempted to use the elevator, he still dragged himself up the stairs to his office. He has never yet used that elevator.

With that kind of determination . . . well, look what has happened to his stock!

One thing I admire about my neighbor, an atheist, is that he mows with an old-fashioned push mower, or reel mower. One hot summer day I offered to let him use mine. No thanks, he said. I knew that was how he would reply, but I still had to tease him.

Everyone believes in calisthenics for the body, even if we don't do them. But nobody seems to believe in calisthenics for the spirit. Nothing in our culture encourages us to exercise our soul.

Jesus in Luke provides us with some daily calisthenics for the soul. Designed to strengthen the spiritual muscles, they require some exertion. But they make us strong and keep us strong for when the really hard times come. We call them spiritual disciplines.

One such spiritual discipline is prayer. Another is fasting. A third is giving to the poor. But I want to concentrate here on loving our enemies as one of the most important.

Loving our enemies is like flexing our spirit. If you want wings, Jesus says, then start flexing the wings of your soul—because otherwise you will only lose what elasticity you have, making it only harder to fly spiritually.

If we can't love our enemies, then we can never really love God, and for sure we can never be like Him. Nor can we ever understand Him. And we will grow weak in spirit.

Jeremiah 12:5 says: "If racing against mere men makes you tired, how will you race against horses? If you stumble and fall on open ground, what will you do in the thickets near the Jordan?" (NLT).

So if you find it hard to get to church now, what will happen when there's a law against it? If you can't treat your spouse in a loving way, how can you love your deadliest enemy? If you can't stay pure at home, what will happen when you find yourself in a foreign environment? Or if you can't give God the time of day when it's easy, what will happen when you have no time? But if you exercise those spiritual muscles, even when it's hard, they grow strong.

Something else Jesus says here is to "give to everyone who asks you, and if anyone takes what belongs to you, do not demand it back."

That is not what they taught me in seminary. That's not even wise, as most people understand it. We have people coming by the church all the time seeking handouts. So this is not a theoretical question.

Giving to every panhandler is bad enough; but what if the people who asked you for money were your enemies? Now that's just plain hard. The people listening to Jesus must have started to mutter and shake their heads. You didn't really mean what You just said, did You?

You mean that if the bank repossesses my car, I should have it washed and polished before handing it over? If a thief steals my silverware, and the police catch him and bring him back to me to identify, should I explain it was a gift and throw in the silver candlesticks, too? Jesus, You can't mean that! (If you are clever, you just recognized this life-changing incident from *Les Misérables*.)

Jesus expands upon what He has just said: "If you love those who love you, what credit is that to you? Even sinners love those who love them. And if you do good to those who are good to you, what credit is that to you? Even sinners do that. And if you lend to those from whom you expect repayment, what credit is that to you? Even sinners lend to sinners, expecting to be repaid in full. But love your enemies, do good to them, and lend to them without expecting to get anything back" (Luke 6:32-35, NIV).

"Look," Jesus is saying. "If you are running in the Olympics, then practice by running uphill with weights on your feet. Do the hard thing. If you really want to bathe in the love of God, then love your enemies." That's what God did. While we were still sinners, Christ died for us (see Rom. 5:8). And then comes the promise: "Then your reward will be great, and you will be children of the Most High, because he is kind to the ungrateful and wicked. Be merciful, just as your Father is merciful" (Luke 6:35, 36, NIV).

What you toss out at the universe is what you will get back, Jesus explains. You want My richest blessings? You want deep fellowship with Me? Then do what I do: Love your enemies.

Life is like a boomerang. What we throw out at others flies back at us, like karma. And so He offers us a plan: "Do not judge, and you will not be judged. Do not condemn, and you will not be condemned. Forgive, and you will be forgiven. Give, and it will be given to you. A good measure, pressed down, shaken together and running over, will be poured into your lap. For with the measure you use, it will be measured to you" (verses 37, 38, NIV).

I used to be a stingy tipper. On occasion I forget this principle and thus still am. It doesn't just work in church, you know. Generosity is how God made the universe to work. So tip your server well.

Let's see, how else does this apply? When you hire workers, offer them a little more than you promised. Surprise people with grace!

Be honest with God. Again and again I have seen newly baptized believers advance from financial weakness to strength, or go from financial weakness to disaster, depending on whether they were faithful in tithing. That's another spiritual exercise.

But it's not just money. It's also the rule of grace. You get what you give. "Judgment without mercy will be shown to anyone who has not been merciful. Mercy triumphs over judgment" (James 2:13, NIV). That's James' summary of the parable of the two debtors.

So be careful with criticisms, because you may get yourself in hot water. It's because we never know the whole story that Jesus told us not to judge others. "Why do you look at the speck of sawdust in your brother's eye and pay no attention to the plank in your own eye? How can you say to your brother, 'Brother, let me take the speck out of your eye,' when you yourself fail to see the plank in your own eye? You hypocrite, first take the plank out of your eye, and then you will see clearly to remove the speck from your brother's eye" (Luke 6:41, 42, NIV).

Our own sins, our little peccadilloes, our slight imperfections, always appear less important to us than the great big blunders of others. But that's a problem with our perspective.

We have an extraordinary spring in the city park near where I live. I've been there when it has been clean, and I've been there when it has been clogged with leaves. Somebody has to get down in the muck and remove the decay of winter. Then it runs clear again.

The water of the gospel is crystal-clear clean as it comes to us through the Word, but it has to flow through polluted channels—namely us. We need to clean them. Do that, and you will find all types of things: love of money, lust, envy, sloth, gluttony, impure media content, evil music, all polluting the flow. They all have to go.

I have a neighbor who frequently had to clear out his fish pond because he had no filter on his circulating pump. Now that he has a filter, he doesn't have to remove the debris as often. Maybe we need to update our moral filters.

Instead of looking for things to criticize in others we should see the faults in ourselves and clean up our own act. Our words then will be the outflow of a loving and pure heart, and we will stop offending people. "No good tree bears bad fruit, nor does a bad tree bear good fruit. Each tree is recognized by its own fruit. People do not pick figs from thornbushes, or grapes from briers. A good man brings good things out of the good stored up in his heart, and an evil man brings evil things out of the evil stored up in his heart. For the mouth speaks what the heart is full of" (verses 43-45, NIV).

Jesus put His finger on the root of our problem. We either have been storing up good things or evil ones. Which way is it with you? Do you remember all the evil things the other side has ever done? Do you like to count all the injustices done to you? Or do you collect beautiful things on the bookshelves of your mind to share with others? The mouth speaks what the heart is full of. Are you filled with complaint or praise?

Proverbs 23:7 reads: "As [a man] thinks within himself, so he is" (HCSB). So sanitize your mind-set of all bitterness, wrath, pride, arrogance, haughtiness, envy, jealousy, and prejudice, and an unforgiving spirit—even toward enemies. Replace those thoughts with grace and love toward everyone.

But that demands a radical cleaning beyond our ability. We need a professional with all the right equipment and chemicals. He will do what we cannot: wash us on the inside. Then His living water can flow pure again through us. His promise is, "Whoever believes in me, as Scripture has said, rivers of living water will flow from within them" (John 7:38, NIV).

# CHAPTER 5

# Jesus and the Sabbath

If Jesus had ever said anything about a change of the Sabbath, we would expect to find it in Luke. Why? Because Luke assisted Paul in his mission to the Gentiles and may have been a Gentile himself. If Jesus ever even hinted that the Gentiles need not keep the Sabbath, Luke would surely mention it. What we find, instead, is that Jesus' custom was to go to the synagogue on the Sabbath (Luke 4:16). Also He relaxed some of the strict Pharisaic rules that encumbered the Sabbath. In particular He repudiated their strictures against relieving suffering on that day (Luke 6:1-11; 13:10-17; 14:1-6).

Finally, Luke mentions that the women who came with Jesus from Galilee "rested the Sabbath day according to the commandment" (Luke 23:56). And right here, just where he would most likely mention any change of the Sabbath commandment, we discover no hint of any such thing, even though Luke was writing many years after the events.

Nevertheless, in the past few decades critical voices have asserted that the Apostolic Council of Acts 15 did away with the Sabbath. After all, the commands it decided upon as binding upon the Gentiles do not include the Sabbath. But before we jump to any conclusion, let's see what secrets lie hidden in Luke's record.

Acts 15 describes a meeting of the leadership of the early church to settle a festering controversy. According to Acts 15:1, 2, "Certain people came down from Judea to Antioch and were teaching the believers: 'Unless you are circumcised, according to the custom taught by Moses, you cannot be saved.' . . . So Paul and Barnabas were appointed, along with some other believers, to go up to Jerusalem to see the apostles and elders about this question" (NIV).

About this time Jewish circles debated the issue of the circumcision of Jewish proselytes. Josephus tells the story of Helena, queen of Adiabene, and her son Izates who embraced Judaism under the influence of a Jewish merchant named Ananias. King Izates feared that his subjects would not accept him if he submitted to circumcision. Ananias assured the king that circumcision was not the most important thing:

> The king could, he [Ananias] said, worship God even without being circumcised if indeed he had fully decided to be a devoted adherent of Judaism, for it was this that counted more than circumcision. He told him, furthermore, that God Himself would pardon him if, constrained thus by necessity and by fear of his subjects, he failed to perform this rite. And so, for the time, the king was convinced by his arguments. Afterwards, however, since he had not completely given up his desire, another Jew, named Eleazar, who came from Galilee and who had a reputation for being extremely strict when it came to the ancestral laws, urged him to carry out the rite.[1]

Notice that various Jewish agents traveled about the empire, some from the school of Hillel who advocated a lax policy on circumcision of proselytes, or Gentile converts, while others from the school of Shammai advocated a strict one. It wasn't just a Christian controversy. This tells us that ignoring circumcision for adult converts did not imply wholesale rejection of the Jewish law.

Paul wrestled with the issue in some of his churches. The Jerusalem council took up the issue about A.D. 45. After much discussion, speeches by Peter and James crystallized the consensus of the group, which they then put into written form. It commanded the Gentiles "to abstain from food sacrificed to idols, from blood, from the meat of strangled animals and from sexual immorality" (Acts 15:29, NIV). It was a rule, not a suggestion—the early church was mainly hierarchical, not congregational—and so Paul and Timothy delivered to the churches in writing the decisions reached by the apostles and elders for them to observe (Acts 16:4, NIV).

But what reasoning process did the apostles follow to arrive at their conclusion? Under the direction of the Holy Spirit (Acts 15:28) they based their decision on a passage in the Torah that laid down laws that applied to non-Jews (variously translated "foreigners," "aliens," or "strangers" in English, or *proselytoi* in Greek) who lived among the Jews. Notice how the decree of Acts 15:29 follows Leviticus exactly, in precise textual order. Notice also that each segment of Leviticus repeats that the law applies to non-Jews:

*"You are to abstain from food sacrificed to idols"* is from Leviticus 17:7-9 (" 'They must no longer offer any of their sacrifices to the goat idols to whom they prostitute themselves. This is to be a lasting ordinance for them and for

the generations to come.' Say to them: 'Any Israelite *or any foreigner residing among them* who offers a burnt offering or sacrifice and does not bring it to the entrance to the tent of meeting to sacrifice it to the Lord must be cut off from the people of Israel' " [NIV]).

*"From blood"* is from Leviticus 17:10 ("I will set my face against any Israelite or *any foreigner residing among them* who eats blood, and cut them off from the people" [NIV]).

*"From the meat of strangled animals"* is from Leviticus 17:15, 16 ("Anyone, whether native-born *or foreigner*, who eats anything found dead or torn by wild animals must wash their clothes and bathe with water, and they will be ceremonially unclean till evening; then they will be clean. But if they do not wash their clothes and bathe themselves, they will be held responsible" [NIV]).

*"And from sexual immorality"* is from Leviticus 18:1-26 ("The Lord said to Moses, 'Speak to the Israelites and say to them: "I am the Lord your God. You must not do as they do in Egypt. . . . No one is to approach any close relative to have sexual relations. I am the Lord. Do not dishonor your father by having sexual relations with your mother. . . . Do not have sexual relations with a man as one does with a woman; that is detestable. Do not have sexual relations with an animal. . . . The native-born *and the foreigners residing among you* must not do any of these detestable things" ' " [NIV]).

The rationale for these rules is obvious: The laws of Leviticus 17 and 18 explicitly state that they apply to Gentile proselytes. The word translated "foreigner" in Leviticus is the Greek *proselytos* in the LXX. So when the church discussed what laws should apply to proselytes, they found a passage that addressed that very question in the law of Moses. Their rules are a simple reading of the Torah, arranged in the same order as the Torah passage.

One might think that the apostolic decree was merely preliminary, provisional, or temporary. Not so. We find it upheld in the letters to the seven churches. "Nevertheless, I have a few things against you: There are some among you who hold to the teaching of Balaam, who taught Balak to entice the Israelites to sin *so that they ate food sacrificed to idols and committed sexual immorality*" (Rev. 2:14, NIV; see also verse 20). By twice citing the first and last stipulations of the apostolic decree of Acts 15:29 John implies the binding nature of the whole. We have no doubt that the apostolic decree stands behind the text, for Revelation 2:24 alludes to it yet again ("I will put upon you none other burden"; cf. Acts 15:28). Evidently some Christians at the end of the first century did not any longer consider the apostolic decree as valid, and John regarded them as heretical.

John's position prevailed in the second-century church. The Didache, sort of an early Christian "church manual" written about A.D. 100, says: "Keep strictly away from meat sacrificed to idols, for it involves the worship of dead gods" (Didache 6:3). Justin Martyr claimed that Christians "abide every torture and vengeance even to the extremity of death, rather than worship idols, or eat meat offered to idols."[2] Eusebius regarded the teaching that there was no harm in eating things sacrificed to idols as a heresy of Basilidies.[3] In the second half of the second century Christians were still not allowed to eat the blood of animals.[4] Finally, all of the bishops of the Christian church, up until the capture of Jerusalem by Hadrian about A.D. 135, were Jewish,[5] not Gentile, and so would be expected to enforce the apostolic decree. The evidence suggests that the church still considered the apostolic decree as normative well after the completion of the New Testament.

Now just what does this decision mean for us today? Well, not everyone is going to be happy about this, because we now leave history and go to meddlin'.

It means that Christians should not eat nonkosher meat. Believers who do so violate the very first decision of the early church in "General Conference" session, a rule approved by the Holy Spirit and never set aside by the church.

* * *

By the way, the apostles themselves set an even higher standard: They didn't eat meat at all. They were vegetarians. Well, at least pesco-vegetarians. They ate fish but not meat.

And just how do we know that?

Jesus' culture considered meat a luxury food, one restricted to special occasions. The normal diet of the Jesus group was bread and fish (Mark 6:38-44; 8:6-9, 14-21; Matt. 7:9, 10; Luke 24:41-43; John 21:9-13). Curiously, Jesus was born in "Beth-lehem," "house of bread," and ministered in "Beth-saida," "house of fish."

Eusebius in about A.D. 310, had this to say about the diet of the apostles: "Consider the character of the disciples of Jesus. . . . They embraced and persevered in a strenuous and a laborious life, with fasting and abstinence from wine and meat, and much bodily restriction besides, with prayers and intercessions to God, and, last but not least, excessive purity, and devotion both of body and soul."[6]

A number of even-earlier Christian writers agree with Eusebius that the apostles abstained from meat and wine. Hegesippus says that James was "holy from his birth; he drank no wine or intoxicating liquor and ate no animal food."[7] Matthew had a similar diet: "It is far better to be happy than to have your bodies act as graveyards for animals. Accordingly, the apostle Matthew partook of seeds, nuts, and vegetables, without flesh."[8] Peter was also vegetarian, according to the *Clementine Homilies* and *Recognitions*.[9] John the Baptist drank no wine or strong drink (Luke 1:15) and ate no meat (Mark 1:6).

This constellation of witnesses is strongly suggestive. If Jesus' half brother James and His cousin John were both vegetarians and teetotalers, and if His disciples Peter and Matthew were both vegetarians, then what does this imply about His diet? You've just discovered something new about the undiscovered Jesus.

The story of Daniel's abstinence from meat in Daniel 1:8-16 would no doubt have influenced Jesus.

OK, but if the Jesus group ate fish and John locusts (locusts are clean food, Lev. 11:22), then how could we call them vegetarian? The Mishnah states: "If a man vowed to abstain from flesh, he is permitted the flesh of fish and locusts" (Hullin 8:1). This previously overlooked evidence tips the balance, it seems to me, in favor of a pesco-vegetarian Jesus.

Jesus was evidently not dogmatic about not eating meat. If He had ever actually forbidden it, there would have been no debate about it later on. The disciples practiced vegetarianism because society in their time expected any apprentice, or disciple, to follow the master's example in everything. But Luke 10:7, 8 notes that Jesus even told His disciples to "eat what is set before you" when away from home on a mission, which suggests temporary suspension of vegetarian scruples. Paul picked up on this in 1 Corinthians 10:27 to justify an exception to the apostolic rule against eating meat offered to idols (Acts 15:20, 29).

The decline of vegetarianism in later Christianity probably results from Paul's lack of enthusiasm for it. Nevertheless, vegetarianism remained popular in the early church. Church fathers that were vegetarian include Athanasius and his opponent Arius, Clement of Alexandria, Origen, Tertullian, Arnobius, Heironymus, Boniface, Chrysostom, and Basil the Great, as well as certain monastic orders.[10] In the early 400s Augustine, who argues *against* vegetarianism, states that those Christians who "abstain both from flesh and from wine" are "without number."[11]

I suspect that the ancient Roman Catholic and Eastern Orthodox practice of fasting every Friday from meat but not fish is a vestigial memory of Jesus' diet.

When Jesus was born, pious Jews fasted twice a week (Luke 18:12; see also

2 Baruch 12:5, 20:5-21:1; 43:3; 4 Ezra 5:13-20; 6:35). Jesus probably did too, at least as a youth. Christians continued the practice, but at some point near the end of the first century they changed the fast days from Monday and Thursday to Wednesday and Friday (Didache 8:1), both to distinguish themselves from the Jews, and because Christ was betrayed on Wednesday and crucified on Friday. This custom, *jejunia quartae et sextae feriae,* came from the apostles, and the whole Christian world observed it, according to Ephiphanius. One Christian leader who is said to have rigorously observed the Wednesday and Friday fasts is Saint Nicholas (270-343)—Santa Claus to you.

This twice-a-week fast is the best explanation of Romans 14:6: "Whoever regards one day as special does so to the Lord. Whoever eats meat does so to the Lord, for they give thanks to God; and whoever abstains does so to the Lord and gives thanks to God" (NIV). In other words, Paul says abstinence from meat on special fast days is optional.

Through the centuries the church eventually dropped the Wednesday fast, leaving us with a Friday fast that believers celebrated by restricting one's diet in imitation of Jesus, thus doing once a week what He did all the time.

By the way, why are we citing all these extracanonical sources? Well, since they are not part of the Bible, they have no doctrinal authority, but they are of historical interest. In other words, they are a witness to ancient beliefs and practices that shed light on the undiscovered Jesus.

But wait. If Jesus was a pesco-vegetarian, then what about the Passover lamb? Jews regarded it as an essential requirement. Of course, they considered marriage as essential for any Jewish male, too, yet Jesus not only practiced celibacy but encouraged others to do so: "There are those who choose to live like eunuchs for the sake of the kingdom of heaven. The one who can accept this should accept it" (Matt. 19:12, NIV). Jesus did not always follow religious norms.

Several pieces of evidence suggest that there was no lamb at the Last Supper.

First, it is hard to see how the central element of the traditional Passover, the Paschal lamb, could have dropped out of the Christian Eucharist tradition without a trace unless it was never there in the first place!

Second, why would Jesus have chosen *vegetarian* symbols (bread and grape juice) to represent His body and blood if actual flesh had been present?

Third, we know that other religious groups had sacred meals without a lamb, such as the mysterious Therapeutae in Egypt, who every seven weeks held a sacred meal, according to Philo: "And the table, too, bears nothing which has blood, but there is placed upon it bread for food and salt for seasoning, to which also hyssop is sometimes added as an extra sauce."[12] Philo's Therapeutae may have been Essenes, or possibly even Christians, as several early Christian writers assert, though scholars doubt it.

The Essenes themselves were probably vegetarian. Josephus, in *Antiquities*, calls the Essenes—the Dead Sea scroll community—"Pythagorean,"[13] which was the word for vegetarian until 1848, the first documented use of the modern term "vegetarian." An archaeological dig of what may have been an Essene settlement unearthed no animal bones according to a brief article in the May/June 1999 issue of *Archaeology*. So it is likely, though not certain, that the Essenes were vegetarian.

Furthermore, we have no record of Jesus or the apostles ever taking part in Temple sacrifices. Already the prophets denigrated Temple sacrifices (1 Sam. 15:22; Prov. 21:3; Isa. 1:11; Hosea 6:6; Amos 5:21; Micah 6:6-8), and now the situation was worse because the high priest was a Roman political appointee instead of a legitimate Zadokite. We know that the Essenes boycotted the Temple sacrifices. The attitude of Jesus, and the Essenes, too, was "I desire mercy, not sacrifice" (Matt. 9:13; 12:7).

Perhaps one reason Jesus avoided the sacrificial system was that He was unconscious of any personal sin, so He did not require a lamb. At any rate, the Temple was the only place where the Passover lamb could be slain, at least around Jerusalem. So it is likely that both Jesus and the Essenes observed a vegetarian Passover.

Why would Jesus abstain from meat but eat fish? You may be interested to know that the latest findings in the field of nutrition confirm the virtues of a pesco-vegetarian diet. Meat is bad for you, and fish is good—*if* you can find an unpolluted source for your fish. Here's why.

Only recently has science discovered the relationship of the human life span with the length of the telomeres on the ends of every strand of DNA in the body. Multiple studies have shown that meat in the diet decreases telomere length, shortening the life of each cell in the body. The MESA study, for example, involving 840 multiracial Americans, found that the higher the intake of processed meat, the shorter the telomeres.

In contrast, other studies show that eating lots of the omega-3 fatty acids EPA and DHA, found in salmon, trout, sardines, anchovies, and so on, results in longer telomeres within the cell.

Also associated with longer telomeres is the natural miracle-drug vitamin D, and fish is its only significant *dietary* source. The main source of vitamin D is sunlight on skin, but in winter, in northern environments, and among people who stay indoors—an ever-increasing percentage of the population—vitamin D deficiency is widespread and associated with many diseases. It is more likely than not that you are vitamin D deficient right this moment.

So fish from *unpolluted* waters is a health food—if you can find it.

\* \* \*

But enough about fish. One more startling fact about Acts 15 is that the apostolic decree exempted only *Gentile* believers from circumcision. The decree still expected Jewish believers to observe it. This is clear not only from Acts 15 itself but also from Acts 21:20-25, in which James and the elders gently rebuke Paul. To get the point, it may help to read the passage aloud, emphasizing the italicized words: "Then they said to Paul: 'You see, brother, how many thousands of Jews have believed, and all of them are zealous for the law. They have been informed that you teach all the Jews who live among the Gentiles to turn away from Moses, telling them not to circumcise their children or live according to our customs [which is not what was voted]. . . . As for the *Gentile* believers, we have written to *them* our decision that they should abstain from food sacrificed to idols, from blood, from the meat of strangled animals and from sexual immorality'" (NIV).

In other words, James and the elders were chiding Paul for allegedly teaching *Jewish* Christians outside of Judea that they were no longer bound by the law of circumcision (Acts 21:21), in violation of the agreement of Acts 15:19, which exempted only *Gentile* Christians (verse 25). This explains the elders' request to Paul in Acts 21:23-27 to sponsor four Jewish believers in observing a vow (probably the Nazirite, see Numbers 6) in order to reassure the critics that Paul, a Jew, was "living in obedience to the law" (verse 24, NIV).

Were the rumors about Paul true? It isn't quite clear, because he held that "circumcision is nothing and uncircumcision is nothing" (1 Cor. 7:19; cf. Gal. 5:6; 6:15). However, in his favor, he kept a Nazirite vow on his own initiative (Acts 18:18), and later he made sure he was ceremonially pure before entering the Temple (Acts 24:18), so we know that Paul was Torah-observant. His acquiescence to the elders (Acts 21:26) and his earlier circumcision of Timothy (Acts 16:3) show submission to church leadership. So Paul himself observed the ritual law, at least when among Jews (1 Cor. 9:20). And he supported in principle the prohibition against meat offered to idols (1 Cor. 10:14-21), although he created a major loophole when the origin of the meat was uncertain (verses 25-28).

The founders of Christianity did not expect their fellow Jews to abandon their heritage when they accepted Jesus. Indeed, the earliest Christians considered themselves not as a separate religion, but as a sect of the Jews known as "the Way." Paul regarded Christianity as fulfilled Judaism, and even Gentiles who believed in Jesus as true Jews: "It is we who are the circumcision" (Phil. 3:3, NIV). "A person is not a Jew who is one only outwardly, nor is circumcision merely outward and physical. No, a person is a Jew who is one inwardly; and circumcision is circumcision of the heart, by the Spirit, not by the written code" (Rom. 2:28, 29, NIV). "It is not the children of the flesh who are the children of God, but the children of the promise are counted as offspring" (Rom. 9:8, ESV). "Those who have faith are children of Abraham" (Gal. 3:7, NIV). "If you belong to Christ, then you are Abraham's seed, and heirs according to the promise" (verse 29, NIV). In other words, authentic Judaism was now Christianity.

According to Brent Kinman, "In recent scholarship on Luke/Acts the essential unity of Israel and the church has been emphasized by defining Israel as an entity consisting of those Jews and Gentiles who believed Jesus to be the Messiah. Israel has been redefined so as both to incorporate believing Gentiles and to exclude ethnic Jews who do not believe."[14]

Since the apostles saw the church as the legitimate continuation of God's covenant people, they quite naturally adopted their canon. They did not discard the Jewish Scriptures and start from scratch. The only things they abandoned were certain "external regulations applying until the time of the new order" (Heb. 9:10, NIV).

Christianity derives from the Old Testament. Christian evangelists did not preach from Christian texts before the destruction of Jerusalem at the earliest, and probably not until the second century. Instead they based their preaching on the Jewish canon. The apostles would have been astonished by the modern evangelical notion that nothing in the Old Testament is binding except whatever the New Testament repeats. Paul writes that "all [Old Testament] Scripture . . . is useful for teaching" (2 Tim. 3:16, NIV). "Do we, then, nullify the law by this faith?" he asks. "Not at all! Rather, we uphold the law" (Rom. 3:31, NIV). Luke, Paul's disciple, records the words of Jesus: "It is easier for heaven and earth to disappear than for the least stroke of a pen to drop out of the Law" (Luke 16:17, NIV). He also chronicles Paul's testimony in a Roman court of law: "I believe everything that is in accordance with the Law and that is written in the Prophets" (Acts 24:14, NIV). And remember that the church's leaders based the decision of Acts 15 on a passage that modern Christians might consider as being part of the ceremonial law.

The church leadership could not have intended to set aside the Torah in

Acts 15, *because they based their decision on the Torah itself.* But if so, then how could they dispense with circumcision for Gentiles? Notice that the covenant God made with Abraham in Genesis 17:10-14, which commands circumcision, is said to apply only to the descendants of Abraham and their slaves—not to the aliens (proselytes) living among them. Exodus 12:43-48 implies that aliens living among the Jews were not normally circumcised unless they wanted to partake in the Passover celebration.

\* \* \*

And now for the final all-important question: Whatever happened to the Decalogue? Acts 15 does not mention the Ten Commandments. The apostolic command to abstain from fornication (*porneia*) refers, as we have seen, to Leviticus 18—not to the seventh commandment, which forbids adultery (*moicheia*). Jewish Greek literature uses these two distinct terms rather consistently, rarely applying the word *porneia* to the seventh commandment. So if the apostolic decree does not mention any of the Ten Commandments—not even the seventh—then does that mean that the Decalogue was no longer binding on Christians?

In other words, did the apostolic council assume that it was now perfectly proper for Gentile Christians to worship other gods, take God's name in vain, break the Sabbath, kill, steal, commit adultery, bear false witness, and so on?

This is obviously absurd. Clearly all parties took for granted the continuing obligation of basic ethical duties enshrined in the Decalogue, which explains the many prescriptive allusions throughout the New Testament—from the words of Jesus in Matthew 19:17, "If you want to enter life, keep the commandments" (NIV), to the description of the saints in Revelation 14:12 as those "who keep the commandments of God, and the faith of Jesus."

Remember that the leader of the council was Jesus' brother James, who had the highest regard for the law. This is clear not only from his dialogue with Paul in Acts 21 but also from his epistle, in which he calls the Decalogue the "perfect law," the "law of freedom," and cites specific commandments in James 1:25; 2:8-12; 4:2, 4, 11; 5:12. James the Just, whom both Josephus[15] and Christian tradition remember as a pious conservative, a vegetarian and a teetotaler, would never have supported any move to lessen the authority of the Decalogue. Nor would he have tolerated a position that abrogated any one particular commandment as having some sort of special obsolete ceremonial status, another modern evangelical notion with no New Testament support.

The basic, primordial rules of morality and worship enshrined in the Ten

Commandments are universal principles going back to Creation. Therefore they apply to all people, not just the Jews. Genesis 26:5 says that Abraham kept "my commandments, my statutes, and my laws." It is certain that the Sabbath, which originated in Eden, was one of those laws on the basis of Genesis 2:3, Exodus 20:11, and Exodus 16:23-30. Particularly interesting is Exodus 16:28, 29, in which God says: "How long will you refuse to keep my commands and my instructions? Bear in mind that the Lord has given you the Sabbath" (NIV). Since the incident happened before Sinai, the Sabbath law clearly preceded the giving of the law on Sinai.

Sabbath is a Creation law, and the Jesus movement held Creation laws in high esteem. The theology of Jesus tended toward restorationism ("back to Eden"), in which precedents from Genesis preempted later legislation. For example, Jesus, in Mark 10:2-12, dismisses a Mosaic law allowing divorce by arguing for the priority of the Creation ordinance of marriage. In Matthew 22:23-32 Jesus again trumps a law of Moses by citing an earlier patriarchal tradition from Genesis (cf. John 7:22). A third example is when Jesus defends the fifth commandment against later Jewish legislation that nullifies it in Mark 7:8-13.

Since Jesus tended to exalt Creation law over later Mosaic legislation, it is unlikely that His followers would have turned their backs on the Sabbath. It is no more reasonable to assume that the apostolic council abrogated the Sabbath than to conclude that it abrogated another Edenic command also omitted from the stipulations of Acts 15—marriage! The Creation laws that antedated Moses were simply not under discussion.

Any decision to change the day of rest would have generated so much controversy as to make the circumcision debate look like a tempest in a teapot— just compare the relative amount of attention given to both commands in the Old Testament. Yet we have no record of such contention.

Keeping the Sabbath in the first century was no more of a problem than it is today. Roman emperors routinely issued decrees allowing Jews to celebrate the Sabbath in peace. Josephus cites some of them in *Antiquities* (book 14, line 10). The Romans did not require Jews to serve in the army, for example.

Indeed, the Sabbath had become an accepted part of life in the Roman Empire. The Romans widely accepted *dies Saturni* as the day of rest. According to Josephus: "The masses have long since shown a keen desire to adopt our religious observances; and there is not one city, Greek or barbarian, nor a single nation, to which our custom of abstaining from work on the seventh day has not spread."[16]

About A.D. 200 Tertullian reproaches pagans for adopting the Jewish custom of resting on the Sabbath: "You have selected one day [Saturday] in preference to other days as the day on which you do not take a bath or you postpone it until the evening, and on which you devote yourselves to leisure and abstain from revelry. In so doing you are turning from your own religion to a foreign religion, for the Sabbath and *cena pura* [special supper] are Jewish ceremonial observances."[17]

After the council of Acts 15, Paul still continued to worship on the Sabbath (Acts 17:1, 2; 18:4), even where there was no Jewish synagogue (Acts 16:13).

The earliest Sabbath controversy I know of in the Christian era is the persecution of the Jews at Antioch about A.D. 66 by one Antiochus, a Jewish renegade who "domineered with severity over his Jewish fellow-citizens, not permitting them to repose on the seventh day, but compelling them to do everything exactly as on other days" so that "not only at Antioch was the weekly day of rest abolished, but the example . . . spread . . . to the other cities as well."[18]

I suppose someone might venture to argue that this was the incident that marked the beginning of the transition to Sunday observance on the part of the Christian church. Even if it did, it occurred after the deaths of James, Peter, and Paul. Not even John, who survived this event by decades, has anything to say about a change in the day of worship.

The council of Acts 15, then, concluded that while not all the laws of Moses were binding on Gentiles, *those laws pertaining to strangers "within thy gates" were still binding—and that would include the Sabbath, according to Exodus 20:10!* The fourth commandment explicitly applies to Gentiles as well as Jews: "The seventh day is the sabbath of the Lord thy God: in it thou shalt not do any work, thou, . . . *nor thy strangers that is within thy gates*" (i.e., "in your towns," the gates belong to a city).

In both Hebrew (*ger*) and Greek (*proselytos*) the word for "stranger" here is the same as in Leviticus 17 and 18—the passage that formed the basis for the Acts 15 decision. *The fourth commandment requires Gentile proselytes to observe the Sabbath.* Two other passages that assert the Sabbath is for Gentiles are Exodus 23:12 and Isaiah 56:6, 7.

So the only one of the Ten Commandments that we can say with certainty that is binding on Gentile believers is the Sabbath!

The Christian church did set aside one class of laws that did apply to strangers or aliens. The law of Moses required the alien to participate in the ritual sacrifices (Num. 15:27-29; 19:10) and the annual festivals closely tied to them (Lev. 16:29; Deut. 16:11, 14). Yet the early Christians, along with other reform movements within Judaism, held that the Jewish sacrificial services were no longer acceptable to God. Hebrews 10:8, 9 explicitly states that God "sets aside" the "sacrifices and offerings, burnt offerings and sin offerings" (NIV). The death of Jesus, the Lamb of God, made the sacrifices obsolete. But they did not abrogate the laws of Leviticus 17 and 18 or the Sabbath.

In summary, the council held that those parts of the Torah that applied to proselytes, with the exception of the sacrificial service, also pertained to Gentile Christians—and the fourth commandment explicitly says that the Sabbath applies to proselytes. We may safely conclude that the apostles and their Gentile converts continued to keep the seventh-day Sabbath after the apostolic council of Acts 15.

*  *  *

Now let's take the long view. The two great institutions that have come down to us over the millennia from Eden are marriage and the Sabbath. The most primitive traditions known to humanity predate sin itself. They are God's gift to us. Interestingly, those primordial institutions have given us just about the only words that are similar in almost all languages.

The word for the seventh day of the week (Saturday in English) in most languages is some variation on the root *sbt* or *spt: Shabbatho, Sabatu, Shapat, Shabati, Sabtu, sabtun, assabt, Sabado,* and so on. The same root underlies our prefix for seven (*sept*uplets, *sept*et, *Sept*ember, once the seventh month, just before *Oct*ober, once the eighth).

In regard to marriage and family, we have the words for "mother" and "father," the first words learned by an infant. The word for mother in most languages involves some variation of the *m* sound plus the vowel *a*: mom, mama, emma, mater, madre. *Mammal* is another derivative, and so is our sound for comfort and savoriness—*mmm*—the closest thing to human purring. And is it mere coincidence that the Hindu mantra is "om"?

The universal words for father usually contain the vowel *a* with a plosive (usually d, p, or b): *daddy, papa, baba, babbo, abba.*

Father, Mother, and Sabbath are human archetypes. They take us right back into Eden.

The Sabbath and marriage are essential to the stability of society. Yet both institutions are under unprecedented attack today. We cannot afford to lose these gifts of God, because without them we are something less than fully human. Their disappearance might suggest a world no longer redeemable.

But God does have a group of worshipers who, individually and corporately, are dedicated to the preservation of these echoes of Eden. They "keep the commandments of God" as found in the Jewish Scriptures—as the apostles did—*and* have "the faith of Jesus" (Rev. 14:12). It's a calling worth the dedication of an entire life.

---

1. Josephus, *Antiquities of the Jews* 20.41-43.

2. Justin Martyr, *Dialogue With Trypho* 34.

3. Eusebius, *The History of the Church From Christ to Constantine* (Minneapolis: Augsburg Pub. House, 1965), p. 159.

4. Ibid., p. 197.

5. Ibid., pp. 156, 157.

6. Eusebius, *Domonstratio Evangelica* 3.5.

7. Eusebius, *The History of the Church*, p. 100.

8. Clement, *The Instructor* 2.1.

9. Clement, *Clementine Homilies*, 12.6; Clement, *Recognitions* 7.1.

10. Jo Ann Davidson, "World Religions and the Vegetarian Diet," *Perspective Digest* 12 (2007): 25-39.

11. Augustine, *Of the Morals of the Catholic Church*, chap. 33.

12. Philo, *De Vita Contemplativa* 9.73, 74.

13. Josephus, *Antiquities* 15.371.

14. Brent Kinman, "Lucan Eschatology and the Missing Fig Tree," *Journal of Biblical Literature* 113 (1994): 675.

15. Josephus, *Antiquities* 20.200, 201.

16. Josephus, *Against Apion* 2.282.

17. Tertullian, *Ad Nationes* 13.

18. Josephus, *Wars of the Jews* 7.52, 53.

# CHAPTER 6

# Jesus and Death

Luke has some special passages that relate to the question of what happens to the dead, still a burning question today. Let's see if we can find something new in Luke.

Many have misunderstood Jesus' story of the rich man and Lazarus (Luke 16:19-31) as teaching that hell is burning now. We can be certain that this story is a parable rather than a factual account, because Luke's introductory wording is one that he always uses for parables. The tell-tale phrase is "a certain so-and-so," using the Greek word *tis,* found at the beginning of parables in Luke 14:16; 15:11; 16:1, 19; 18:2; 19:12.

It is always hazardous to base a theological belief on the incidental details of a parable. Otherwise the previous parable to this one would appear to recommend dishonest behavior. We should not use the parable in Judges 9:8-15 about talking plants to prove that plants can talk. Nor should we cite Jesus' short parable about the mustard seed in Matthew 13:31, 32 as proof that the mustard is the smallest of all seeds (it is not). Likewise, here Jesus did not tell His story to teach that the dead are suffering now. The essential elements of the story of the rich man and Lazarus were already part of popular Jewish folklore in the time of Christ, who borrowed them to make a point about the use of money and how it affects our destiny.

Parables involve exaggeration. Taking them literally leads us into a labyrinth of confusion. Servants do not literally live off crumbs from their masters' table. Nor do the righteous converse with their tormented loved ones throughout eternity. The righteous dead are not in Abraham's literal bosom any more than they are literally under an altar (Rev. 6:9-11). These are figures of speech. When our friends say "I am so hungry I could eat a horse," we do not accuse them of lying because the statement is not literally true. We are more likely to say "Me too."

So far everything in this chapter is old hat. But "old hat" is not good enough. We need something new. I will not waste your time by merely re-stating the tradition. Remember what Jesus says in Matthew 13:52: "Every teacher of the law who has become a disciple in the kingdom of heaven is like the owner of a house who brings out of his storeroom new treasures as well as old" (NIV). No pastor or teacher should neglect to do this, particularly now that research is easier than ever with the Internet.

There has to be a balance. Too much new without the old is disruptive, while too much old without the new is boring. So here, then, is something new for you.

As it turns out, some scholars have found another layer of meaning in this parable besides the appeal to good stewardship. The name Lazarus is the Greek form of the Jewish name Eleazar/Eliezar/Eliezer (just as Jesus is the Greek form of Joshua, or James the Greek form of Jacob, or Sadducee is the Greek form of Zadokite). As long ago as 1868 someone suggested that the Lazarus of the parable is the chief steward of Abraham named in Genesis 15:2.[1] This interpretation sheds a flood of light on the parable.

The phrase "desiring to be fed with the crumbs which fell from the rich man's table" (Luke 16:21) suggests that Eliezer was a Gentile (cf. Matt. 15:22-28), as does the phrase "laid at his gate" (Luke 16:20), which is similar to the phrase used of Gentile proselytes, "proselyte of the gate."

In Jewish tradition, Eliezer was a Gentile. In addition, Eliezer is somehow associated with stewardship—the theme of the parable—and with Abraham. Only one Eliezer in the Bible fits the description: Eliezer of Damascus, a Gentile, and the chief steward (manager) of Abraham.

In contrast to the unfaithful steward of the preceding parable in Luke 16:1-13, Eliezer was a faithful steward in that his first concern was for the welfare of his master, even at his own expense. Although he was the legal heir to all of Abraham's possessions (Gen. 15:3), Abraham assigned him to find a wife for his son (Gen. 24:3). Now Eliezer would have had a strong disincentive to do this, because it would have resulted in his own disinheritance. Nevertheless, he carried out the orders of Abraham faithfully, even though it meant that Isaac would inherit everything, leaving him with nothing (verse 36). Now Eliezer was rejected as an heir. Thus, the parable portrays Lazarus as a "beggar" with nothing of earthly worth.

Who then was the rich man of the parable, who called Abraham "father" (Luke 16:24) and whom Abraham called "son" (verse 25), who wore purple, the symbol of kingship (cf. Gen. 49:10), and *who had five brothers* (verse 28)? He can only be Judah, who gave the Jews their name. Judah's mother, Leah, bore Jacob six sons (Gen. 30:20). His five brothers were Reuben, Simeon,

Levi, Issachar, and Zebulun (Gen. 35:23).

What a fantastic quiz question to befuddle even the most expert Bible scholars: What are the real names of the five brothers of the rich man mentioned in Luke 16:28?

As the people of Judah possessed the "oracles of God" (Rom. 3:1, 2), so the rich man and his brothers had in their midst "Moses and the prophets" (Luke 16:29). But in the end, unfaithful Judah—Judaism—received torment, while Eliezer, the faithful Gentile—Gentile Christianity—was received into the "eternal dwellings" (verse 9, NIV). Being in "Abraham's bosom" meant that he was adopted into the family and came into intimate relationship with Abraham (cf. John 1:18, in which Jesus is said to be "in the bosom of the Father").

In other words, many of the Jews would be lost while believing Gentiles would be saved. This parable was important to Luke. First of all, because his mentor, Paul, was the apostle to the Gentiles (Rom. 11:13; Eph. 3:8). But Luke himself may have been a Gentile, or at least a Hellenized Jew, that is, he may have been a "God-fearer," as suggested by Colossians 4:10, 11, 14, and he might have come to study at Jerusalem and encountered Jesus during his lifetime. And note that some scholars think that Luke sees himself in Acts 10:34, 35.

The "great chasm" of the parable (Luke 16:26, NIV) is probably an allusion to the Great Rift Valley, which separates the highlands of Transjordan and the hill country of Ephraim and is the longest visible chasm on earth. It is about 3,700 miles long and runs from northern Syria to central Mozambique. The Jordan River flows at the bottom of this canyon in the Middle East, dividing the land of promise given to Abraham from the land of the Gentiles. To the west side of the Jordan was the Holy Land. When Joshua set foot on it, he was told by an angel, "Take off your sandals, for the place where you are standing is holy" (Joshua 5:15, NIV).

The parable states that no one could "cross over" the chasm (Luke 16:26, NIV)—an allusion to a water crossing. Greek imagery of the abodes of the dead usually places some kind of water barrier between the righteous dead and the wicked—either a river or an ocean. Entering the land of Canaan (west of the Jordan) was a symbol of final spiritual salvation. The author of Hebrews recognized that Israel's crossing of the river Jordan under Joshua (and the taking of the land of Canaan) was a foreshadowing of Christians obtaining their true "rest" in the future kingdom of God (Heb. 3:1-4:11). The American spiritual "Deep River" reflects this symbolic theme.

This parable, then, affirms Gentile Christianity at the expense of Judaism, like other Lukan parables, such as the one about the kind Samaritan versus the haughty priest and Levite (Luke 10:31-33); the fruitless fig tree given one more year before being cut down (Luke 13:8); the banquet whose original guests refuse the invitation and get rejected in favor of the crippled, blind, and lame (Luke 14:24); the lost son who comes home to a celebration versus the older brother who "refused to go in" (Luke 15:28, NIV); the self-righteous Pharisee versus the penitent tax collector (Luke 18:10-14); and the landowner who kills his rebellious tenants and gives the vineyard to others (Luke 20:16). In the parable here the older brother, Judah, refused the gospel message of salvation. He would not be convinced even by one risen from the dead (Luke 16:31)—an obvious reference to Judaism and Jesus' resurrection.

The parable of Lazarus appears only in the book of Luke. Luke resurrected and immortalized this piece of the teaching of Jesus because it provided support for the Gentile mission. It teaches that believing Gentiles may inherit the Abrahamic promises if they are faithful stewards like Eliezer. And it reflects such Pauline themes as that of Galatians 3:29, which describes Gentile Christians as "Abraham's seed and heirs according to the promise," and of Galatians 4:21-31, in which Paul speaks of Abraham's two sons, one by the slave woman and one by the free woman, and of Mount Sinai and Jerusalem (i.e., Judaism is the slave and Christians are the children of promise and sons of the free woman).

* * *

If the parable of the rich man and Lazarus does not speak to what happens after death, another pivotal passage in Luke does. Jesus promises the thief on the cross, "I tell you the truth today you will be with Me in paradise" (see Luke 23:43).

Does the comma go before or after "today"?

What the dying criminal asked was for Jesus to "remember me when you come into your kingdom" (verse 42, NIV). According to Jewish tradition, Paradise with its tree of life would be restored to the righteous on earth in the new age of the kingdom. We find this idea in both Christian and Jewish literature, such as Revelation 2:7 with 22:1, 2; Testament of Levi 18:10; Testament of Dan 5:12; 1 Enoch 25:4; 2 Enoch 65:9, 10; 4 Ezra 7:36, 123; and Apocalypse of Moses 13:2-5; 28:4. The basis for this belief may be Isaiah 51:3 and Ezekiel 36:35. So "when you come into your kingdom" does not mean "as soon as you get to heaven today after you die," as if the thief were a modern evangelical.

But many scholars allege that Jesus gave the thief more than he asked for.

We can translate Jesus' reply in two different ways: the comma may either precede or follow "today." Both translations are correct as far as the Greek is concerned. Based on his Aramaic expertise, George M. Lamsa translates, "Truly I say to you today, you will be with me in Paradise." In support of this rendering is the fact that the expression "I command you today" or some variant is a common idiom that occurs some 35 times in Deuteronomy. Note, for example, Deuteronomy 30:18, LXX, "I declare to you today that you will utterly perish" (*anaggello soi semeron;* cf. Luke 23:43, *soi lego semeron*). Jesus was well acquainted with Deuteronomy, as indicated by His dialogue with Satan during the wilderness temptation, quoting from Deuteronomy 6-8.

Unfortunately, Lamsa's punctuation of Luke 23:43, though possible, is unlikely. No other translation follows Lamsa, because the evidence against it is formidable.

The main problem is that, in Luke, Jesus frequently speaks of things happening "today" in a literal sense: "He began by saying to them, '*Today* this scripture is fulfilled in your hearing' " (Luke 4:21, NIV); "He replied, 'Go tell that fox, "I will keep on driving out demons and healing people *today* and tomorrow, and on the third day I will reach my goal" ' " (Luke 13:32, NIV); "When Jesus reached the spot, he looked up and said to him, 'Zacchaeus, come down immediately. I must stay at your house *today*' " (Luke 19:5, NIV); "Jesus said to him, '*Today* salvation has come to this house, because this man, too, is a son of Abraham' " (verse 9, NIV); "Jesus answered, 'I tell you, Peter, before the rooster crows *today*, you will deny three times that you know me' " (Luke 22:34, NIV). "Jesus answered him, 'I tell you the truth, *today* you will be with me in paradise' " (Luke 23:43, NCV).

When Jesus says "today" in Luke, He means that very day.

Jesus' most common expression, *"amen* I tell you" (translated as "Verily, I say unto you" in the KJV or "I tell you the truth" in the NIV[2]) occurs many times in the Gospels, but never elsewhere in the form, "I tell you the truth *today*." The closest thing to an exception is Mark 14:30, " 'I tell you the truth,' Jesus answered, 'today—yes, tonight, before the rooster crows twice—you yourself will disown me three times' " But this parallel tends to support the traditional rendering of Luke 23:43, since the event did occur literally on that day.

However, even if the traditional placement of the comma in Luke 23:43 is correct, this incident constitutes a special case. Moses, too, seems to have been granted a special resurrection, as implied in Jude 9, Mark 9:4, and apparently described in the apocryphal *Assumption of Moses,* which the New Testament writers may have read but which is no longer extant. But an exceptional case tells us nothing about normal eschatology. Enoch, Moses, and Elijah were also taken to Paradise under extraordinary circumstances. We cannot simply assume that the thief is a paradigm of what happens to all of the righteous at death.

But even a special case interpretation is doubtful, since the resurrected Jesus told Mary, "Do not hold on to me, *for I have not yet ascended to the Father*" (John 20:17, NIV). Matthew 12:40 and Ephesians 4:9, 10 also suggest that Christ was not in heaven during those three days. Jesus could not have met the thief in Paradise on Friday, because God's throne and Paradise are both in the same place: the third heaven (2 Cor. 12:2-4). That God's throne is in Paradise is also implied when we compare Revelation 2:7 with Revelation 22:1, 2.

So the best solution is that Jesus was speaking of a sort of flexible "time" that we could not measure by human clocks. In other words, "Today you shall be with me in paradise" is like "in the day you eat you shall die" (see Gen. 2:17). The thief, *as far as his personal experience was concerned,* would find himself in Paradise after a few more hours of suffering on the cross— even if ages had passed in the interim, because there is no sense of the passage of time in the grave. Eons vanish in an instant.

For those who are dismayed that we have just demolished their favorite argument regarding the thief on the cross, we have something to give back that more than makes up for it. It is another undiscovered truth. We put it here because it establishes the interpretation advocated in the above paragraphs, and at the same time demolishes a misleading argument long based on a passage in Philippians that seems to say that people go to heaven when they die.

Here is the problem passage: "I eagerly expect and hope that . . . Christ will be exalted in my body, whether by life or by death. For to me, to live is Christ and *to die is gain.* If I am to go on living in the body, this will mean fruitful labor for me. Yet what shall I choose? I do not know! I am torn between the two: *I desire to depart and be with Christ,* which is better by far; but it is more necessary for you that I remain in the body. Convinced of this, I know that I will remain, and I will continue with all of you for your progress and joy in the faith" (Phil. 1:20-25, NIV).

This passage has for centuries been a mainstay in the discussion over what happens at death. It certainly sounds as if Paul wants to die and go to heaven immediately, doesn't it?

I was always troubled by this passage until I read Plato's *Apology* and happened upon the phrase "To die is gain."

With the possible exception of Homer's *Iliad* and *Odyssey,* Plato's *Apology* is probably the most famous piece of literature ever written outside of

Scripture. At least it was in Jesus' day. Every well-educated individual had read Plato's *Apology.* Paul was undoubtedly familiar with it. Jesus may have been as well, because in a later chapter we will examine a parallel to Jesus' sermon on the mount.

The word *apologia* in Greek has little to do with apologizing for a wrong. It means "defense." People who defend the Christian faith—or anything else—are known even today as apologists, and the field of study that answers the objections of skeptics against Christianity is referred to as apologetics. Plato's *Apology* is his account of the trial of his teacher Socrates—a legal hearing regarded as perhaps the greatest judicial miscarriage of justice in history until the crucifixion of Jesus. Because Socrates defended himself, Plato's book contained the great philosopher's *apologia.*

Here, then, is the relevant passage. Just after he is condemned to die, Socrates muses on the nature of death:

> Either death is a state of nothingness and utter unconsciousness, or, as men say, there is a change and migration of the soul from this world to another. Now if you suppose that there is no consciousness, but a sleep like the sleep of him who is undisturbed even by the sight of dreams, *death will be an unspeakable gain.* For if a person were to select the night in which his sleep was undisturbed even by dreams, and were to compare with this the other days and nights of his life, and then were to tell us how many days and nights he had passed in the course of his life better and more pleasantly than this one, I think that any man, I will not say a private man, but even the great king, will not find many such days or nights, when compared with the others. Now if death is like this, I say that *to die is gain;* for eternity is then only a single night (italics supplied).

Plato's implication is clear: If the soul sleeps—if an eternity of death is "only a single night"—then to die is gain. This explains Paul's terminology in his letter to Philippi. If the dead in Christ have no sense of the passing of time, but death and resurrection are separated only by the blink of an eye, then as far as their experience is concerned, *to die is to be with Christ.* Accident victims who wake from a deep coma may think it happened only yesterday, even if it was years ago. That is how Paul in Philippians 1:23 can speak of the reunion with Christ as if it were simultaneous with death. And that is what Jesus meant when He told the thief on the cross, "Today you will be with Me in paradise."

In Philippians 1:20-25 Paul does not separate between the departure and the reward, but he does so in 2 Timothy 4:6-8: "The time for my departure is near. . . . Now there is in store for me the crown of righteousness, which the Lord, the righteous Judge, will award to me *on that day*" (NIV). In the New Testament this phrase signifies the day of the Lord (2 Thess. 2:3; 2 Tim. 1:12, 18; see also Matt. 7:22; 24:36; 26:29; Luke 10:12; 17:31; 21:34; 2 Pet. 3:12). That Paul is using the phrase in its normal sense we see indicated by the continuation: "and not only to me, but also to all who have longed for *his appearing*" (2 Tim. 4:8, NIV). It is only after the Second Coming that we are "with the Lord" (1 Thess. 4:17; John 14:3).

Furthermore, we know this is what Paul has in mind when he mentions departing to be with Christ because of what he said a few verses before in Philippians 3:10, 11: "I want to know Christ—yes, to know the power of his resurrection and participation in his sufferings, becoming like him in his death, and so, somehow, *attaining to the resurrection from the dead.*" Here Paul is thinking in terms of the resurrection, which will be only a blink of an eye from the moment of death. So to him, to depart is to be with Christ.

* * *

We find still yet another passage in Luke relevant to our discussion of what happens in death. In Luke 20:37, 38 Jesus says, "But in the account of the burning bush, even Moses showed that the dead rise, for he calls the Lord 'the God of Abraham, and the God of Isaac, and the God of Jacob.' He is not the God of the dead, but of the living, for *to him* all are alive" (NIV).

That is, all are alive as far as the Lord is concerned, because He "gives life to the dead and calls those things *which do not exist as though they did*" (Rom. 4:17, NKJV). Jesus in Luke is speaking proleptically of the resurrection of the dead. Note that the point Christ is trying to prove in dispute with the Sadducees, who did not believe in the resurrection, is not that the dead are still alive but that the dead rise (Luke 20:27).

But why did Jesus use this oblique argument from the Pentateuch instead of just citing a clearer proof text such as Daniel 12:2? The reason is that He was talking to the Sadducees, who accepted only the books of Moses as authoritative. They did not believe in angels or demons, heaven or hell, or the resurrection, because their canon, the Torah, did not mention such things. They were the upper-class, skeptical aristocrats who controlled the high priesthood and the Temple in Jesus' day.

And why did they have control of the Temple? Because they were given charge of it in Ezekiel 40:46; 43:19; 44:15; 48:11. Note that the Septuagint here reads "sons of Sadduc" (Zadok). Ask almost any biblical scholar where the Old Testament mentions the Sadducees, and you will get a blank look. Now you know. The Sadducees are the Zadokites.

This is why the priests are called "sons of Zadok" in the Dead Sea Scrolls. Just as the legitimate king of Israel was to be a son of David, so the legitimate high priest was to be a son of David's high priest, Zadok.

Unfortunately, lots of dirty water had gone under the bridge between the time of Ezekiel and that of Christ. Power and money corrupt, and so does political meddling by higher powers. During the second Temple period the Maccabees had replaced the Zadokite high priesthood with their own, demoting the ethnic Zadokites to a lower position. By Jesus' day the priests were political appointees of Rome and not ethnic Zadokites, a fact that brought the priesthood into disrepute. Almost none of the priests during the Hasmonean, Herodian, and Roman periods were actual descendants of Zadok. Hence such reform movements as that of John the Baptist withdrew from participation in the Temple cultus, which many now saw as illegitimate.

According to Luke, it was the Sadducees, not the Pharisees, who mainly persecuted the early church since they felt threatened by the message that Jesus had risen from the dead. It was the Sadducees who arrested Peter and John (Acts 4:1-3), then all the apostles (Acts 5:17, 18). Sadducees attacked Paul the Pharisee, and the Pharisees defended him (Acts 23:6-9). Many of the new believers were Pharisees (Acts 15:5).

The Pharisees were much closer to the people and (believe it or not) to Jesus in their beliefs than the Sadducees. The reason Jesus argued with the Pharisees more than the Sadducees was that brothers and sisters bicker more than strangers.

But back to Luke 20. I was startled to discover that Jesus was not the first to use this argument from the patriarchs to prove life after death. The same kind of reasoning crops up in other Jewish literature roughly contemporary with Jesus. Philo, who did not believe in a resurrection, used almost the same argument in *De Fuga et Inventione* to conclude that the soul survives death.[3] Fourth Maccabees makes a similar point: "Those who die for the sake of God live to God, as do Abraham and Isaac and Jacob and all the patriarchs" (4 Maccabees 16:25, NRSV); "But as many as attend to religion with a whole heart, these alone are able to control the passions of the flesh, since they believe that they, like our patriarchs Abraham and Isaac and Jacob, do not die to God, but live to God" (4 Maccabees 7:18, 19, NRSV). Notice the exact same phraseology that Jesus used: the patriarchs live "to God."

At first glance such evidence might seem to question the idea that Jesus was talking about the resurrection. After all, Philo and the author of 4 Maccabees use it to prove the survival of the soul after death. *Hmmm.*

But according to H. Anderson,  the author of 4 Maccabees "subscribes to the idea of the immortality of the soul. The great hope expressed in 4 Maccabees is that the pure and immortal soul might enter into the incorruption of life everlasting (9:22; 14:5f.; 16:13; 17:12; 18:23). His espousal of the Greek doctrine of the immortality of the soul is clear-cut and striking; he consistently omits the passages in his primary source, 2 Maccabees, that testify unreservedly to the Jewish belief in the resurrection of the body (7:9, 11, 14, 22f.)."[4]

Did you catch that? Like most Christians today, the writer of 4 Maccabees believes in the immortality of the soul, so he *consistently omits* passages in his source that talk about the resurrection of the body. But Jesus and the New Testament writers, in contrast, speak of the resurrection often. Do you see the implication? An immortal-soul advocate will not mention the resurrection, yet the New Testament is full of such references. What does that imply?

If the righteous go to heaven at death, then no resurrection is needed, since the saints are already enjoying their reward. Acts 17:32 records that when Paul began to talk about resurrection, the Athenians sneered at him—because they understood his teaching to be incompatible with Greek belief of immortality of the soul. They were right, and their derision makes perfect sense. Why would glorified spirits in heaven have any interest in recovering their old earthly bodies that had long since rotted into dust? The very idea is bizarre and repugnant. Even if those resurrected bodies are freed from all pollution and limitations, whatever could be the point of a fleshly resurrection out of the dirt for ethereal spirits? Only if Jesus and Paul taught that there is no human existence apart from the body, and the righteous are asleep in the grave, does physical resurrection make any sense at all. You must pick one or the other: either the soul sleeps and awakens at the final resurrection, or the soul goes to heaven or hell at death. *You cannot have both.* If the New Testament teaches resurrection, then it necessarily assumes the soul sleeps. Period.

All of this suggests that Jesus' words in Luke 20:27 are a conscious metamorphosis of the argument used by Philo and 4 Maccabees. Jesus is adopting a line of argument that the soul transcends death, one that had proven useful against the Sadducees, who did not believe this. But now He was using it to teach "that the dead rise" (Luke 20:37, NIV).

For Jesus and Paul, the resurrection was the only solution to death. Paul taught that dead believers have no hope apart from resurrection. It is the clear implication of 1 Corinthians 15:17, 18: "If Christ has not been raised, your faith is futile; you are still in your sins. Then those also who have fallen asleep in Christ are lost" (NIV) "Lost" here (*apolonto*) means "perished." The same root appears in Matthew 10:28: "Do not be afraid of those who kill the body but cannot kill the soul. Rather, be afraid of the One who can *destroy* both soul and body in hell" (NIV); and twice in 1 Corinthians 1:18, 19: "For the message of the cross is foolishness to those who are *perishing,* but to us who are being saved it is the power of God. For it is written: 'I will *destroy* the wisdom of the wise; the intelligence of the intelligent I will frustrate' " (NIV). *Apolonto* connotes annihilation. Those who have fallen asleep in Christ are gone, perished, destroyed, finished.

Any Greek thinker would have thought that a strange thing to say. The Jewish philosopher Philo, who lived in Alexandria at the same time Jesus lived, would have retorted, Don't be silly! The righteous dead are in the celestial realms. Good men do not die, he declares, but depart. The soul cannot be extinguished, but migrates from earth to heaven.[5] Like the stars, the soul is a fragment of quintessence, and returns to it.[6] The good, even if separated from the body, live forever.[7] A virtuous proselyte will receive a "firm and sure habitation in heaven."[8] Virtue makes the soul immortal, and it attains to heaven.[9]

Josephus records this same belief in the speech given by Eleazar, leader of the Jews at Masada: "Death truly gives liberty to the soul and permits it to depart to its own pure abode, there to be free of all calamity."[10]

Even Roman writers teach the same thing. In the first century B.C. Cicero describes a dream in which Africanus and his father, Paulus, both deceased, give Scipio a tour of the heavens. They tell Scipio,

> Every man who has preserved or defended his country, or has made it greater, is reserved a special place in heaven, where he enjoys an eternal life of happiness. . . . In fact, it is from this place, here, in heaven, that the rulers and preservers of states come from, and to which they eventually return. . . . Unless God, who rules all you see around you here, frees you from your confinement in the body, you cannot gain entrance to this paradise. . . . Love justice and devotion. . . . Such is the life that leads to heaven, and to the company of those who, having finished their lives in the world, are now freed from their bodies and dwell in that region you gaze upon, the Milky Way.[11]

It is probably in reaction to such beliefs that Jesus states in John 3:13 that "no one has ever gone into heaven except the one who came from heaven— the Son of Man" (NIV).

Another Roman writer, Manilius, writes in the first century A.D.: "Perhaps the souls of heroes, outstanding men deemed worthy of heaven, freed from the body and released from the globe of Earth, pass hither and, dwelling in a heaven that is their own, live the infinite years of paradise and enjoy celestial bliss."[12]

Porphyry wrote a book called *Against the Christians.* In a different book (*Life of Plotinus* 22) he wrote about A.D. 300:

> But now that you have cast the screen aside, quitted the tomb [i.e., your body] that held your lofty soul, you enter at once the heavenly consort: where fragrant breezes play, where all is unison and winning tenderness and guileless joy, and the place is lavish of the nectar-streams the unfailing Gods bestow, with the blandishments of the Loves, and delicious airs, and tranquil sky: where . . . Plato, consecrated power, and stately Pythagoras and all else that form the Choir of Immortal Love, that share their parentage with the most blessed spirits, there where the heart is ever lifted in joyous festival. O Blessed One, you have fought your many fights; now, crowned with unfading life, your days are with the Ever-Holy.

It is really quite discouraging that this pagan belief has become standard among Christians today. Modern evangelicals choose the faith of Plato and Philo over that of Jesus and Paul. Amazing!

As far as Paul was concerned, such a belief was not even possible as a fall-back view. The only reprieve from the grave was resurrection. If the apostle had believed that death was the doorway into heaven, as both Romans and Greeks did, then his statement that dead believers were *apolonto* apart from the resurrection of Christ would be nonsense. Likewise nonsensical would be 1 Corinthians 15:32: "If the dead are not raised, 'Let us eat and drink, for tomorrow we die.' " Paul clearly believes that, except for resurrection, *death is the end.*

Let us contrast Paul and Philo on this doctrine. Philo writes, "The death of the good is the beginning of another life; for life is a twofold thing, one life being in the body, corruptible; the other without the body, incorruptible. . . . A good man . . . does not surely die, but has his life prolonged, and so attains to an eternal end."[13]

Contrast Paul's position in 1 Corinthians 15:50-54, which uses some of the same terminology but comes to a very different conclusion: we shall all be changed from corruption to incorruption at the last trumpet, when the dead are raised, "for this corruptible must put on incorruption, and this mortal must put on immortality."

The teaching of Philo, "A good man . . . does not surely die," has an ancient pedigree. It is the first heresy, originating on the lips of the serpent in Eden (Gen. 3:4).

The early church fathers are not always reliable, but usually they knew the difference between truth and error. Justin Martyr, writing about A.D. 160, devotes two chapters of his book *Dialogue With Trypho,* 80 and 81, to this question. First, he makes the point that soul and body cannot possibly exist separately. Then he continues, "Why do we any longer endure those unbelieving arguments, and fail to see that we are regressing when we listen to such an argument as this: That the soul is immortal, but the body mortal, and incapable of being revived. For this we used to hear from Plato, even before we learned the truth. If then the Savior said this and proclaimed salvation to the soul alone, what new thing beyond what we heard from Plato, did He bring us?"

The doctrine that the righteous go to heaven at death, he argues, is heresy. One cannot even consider as Christian those who teach it and thus deny the resurrection: "If you have fallen in with some who are called Christians, but who do not admit this, and venture to blaspheme the God of Abraham, and the God of Isaac, and the God of Jacob; who say there is no resurrection of the dead, and that their souls, when they die, are taken to heaven; do not imagine that they are Christians" (*Trypho* 80).

Another important Christian leader, Irenaeus, writing only a few years later, also denies that the soul enters heaven at death: "For the heretics . . . affirm that immediately upon their death they shall pass above the heavens." Jesus did not go to heaven when He died, but only after His resurrection, Irenaeus continues, and so it is with His saints.[14]

Two other church fathers who deny that Christians go to heaven at death are Hippolytus (*Against Plato, On the Cause of the Universe* 1, 2) and Tertullian (*Treatise on the Soul* 55).

Unfortunately, such writers failed to prevent the intrusion of Greek philosophy into the church. What they called heresy has, alas, become Christian orthodoxy. Seventh-day Adventists are one of the few groups who have consistently opposed the teaching.

---

1. See C. H. Cave, "Lazarus and the Lukan Deuteronomy," *New Testament Studies* 15 (1969): 319-325; Ernest L. Martin, "The Real Meaning of Lazarus and the Rich Man," available online.

2. Wording is from 1984 *New International Version.*

3. Philo, *De Fuga et Inventione* 55-59.

4. H. Anderson, "4 Maccabees," in James H. Charlesworth, ed., *The Old Testament Pseudepigrapha* (Peabody, Mass.: Hendrickson Publishers, 1983), vol. 2, p. 539.

5. Philo, *Quis Rerum Divinarum Heres Sit* 276.

6. Ibid., 283.

7. Philo, *De Fuga* 55.

8. Philo, *De Praemiis et Poenis* 152.

9. Philo, *Quaestiones et Solutiones in Genesin* 1.51.

10. Josephus, *Wars of the Jews* 7.341.

11. Cicero, *The Republic* 6.13ff.

12. Manilius, *Astronomica* 1.758.

13. Philo, *Quaestiones* 1.16.

14. Irenaeus, *Against Heresies* 5.31.

# CHAPTER 7

# The Secret of Jesus' Power

The book of Mark has a puzzling phenomenon. Scholars call it the "Messianic secret." Jesus repeatedly asked those He healed to keep quiet about His miracles (Mark 1:25, 34, 43-45; 3:12; 5:43; 7:36; 8:30; 9:9; etc.). It was sort of an antiadvertising campaign—just the opposite of the way we do it. Why?

One possible answer would be to keep Him alive. He didn't want to draw the attention of the authorities. The rabble were always looking for someone to lead them in revolt. Regarding crowds as politically suspect, the Romans burned, crucified, or beheaded messianic aspirants along with their followers. Accusations of messianic claims could result in a death sentence (Luke 23:2; Acts 17:7). According to Josephus, Herod imprisoned John the Baptist on the mere suspicion that he might eventually lead a rebellion.[1] Yet John worked no miracles (John 10:41) and apparently made no messianic claims—he merely drew crowds. Jesus was much more of a threat. People were touting Him as the Messiah, and He also worked miracles, so He posed a serious threat to the establishment. John 6:15 says Jesus found Himself forced to avoid the enthusiasm of the crowd, who "intended to come and make him king by force" (NIV). He had to lower His profile until His time had come.

But what happened when those He healed ignored His request for silence and spread the news explains the real answer: "Jesus could no longer enter a town openly but stayed outside in lonely places. Yet the people still came to him from everywhere" (Mark 1:45, NIV). Everyone wanted to touch Him (Mark 3:10; 5:28; 6:56), and He struggled to find private time (Mark 1:35-38, 45; 6:31-34, 45, 46, 54-56; John 6:24-27).

To avoid being mobbed Jesus hit on the solution of pushing out from the shore in a small boat as a speaking platform (Mark 3:8-10; 4:1), which gave Him a convenient getaway. Note Matthew 8:18: "When Jesus saw the crowd around him, he gave orders to cross to the other side of the lake" (NIV).

Still, He couldn't hide and had no privacy. "He entered a house and did not want anyone to know it; yet he could not keep his presence secret" (Mark 7:24, NIV). "Jesus did not want anyone to know where they were, because he was teaching his disciples" (Mark 9:30, 31, NIV). Just about the only time Jesus ventured outside of Palestine as an adult (Mark 7:24) was a desperate attempt to hide from the Jews so that He could secure the rest interrupted in Mark 6:30-34, 53-56. The crowds would not follow Him into pagan territory.

Jesus' so-called Messianic secret must have been a desperate attempt to retain some privacy. Successful faith healers or exorcists eventually find that unless they impose some limitations on the endless supply of desperate clients, they will have no time to eat or sleep. As long as services are free of charge, the problem has no easy solution.

Jesus may have loved people, and loved preaching too, but unlike modern faith healers, actors, and politicians, He seems to have disliked crowds. Imagine a modern faith healer who, when told, "Everyone is looking for you!" says, "Well then, let's go somewhere else!" (see Mark 1:37, 38; Matt. 8:18; Luke 4:42, 43). What preacher would not appreciate an instant audience? Why leave one eager crowd to look for another?

And what modern faith healer isolates the sick from the crowd as Jesus often did? Note Mark 5:24: "A large crowd followed and pressed around him." However, "He did not let anyone follow him except Peter, James and John the brother of James" (verse 37, NIV). Arriving at Jairus's house and finding a new crowd of mourners on the scene, "He put them all out" (verse 40, NIV). After He healed the girl, "He gave strict orders not to let anyone know about this" (verse 43, NIV; see also similar accounts in Matt. 9:23-25, 27-30; Mark 7:32, 33; 9:25-28). Why not show off the miracle to as many as possible to build faith? One almost gets the impression that Jesus regarded healing the sick and feeding the hungry as a distraction from His call to preach the kingdom (note Mark 1:38; John 6:24-27).

Jesus seems to have disliked crowds. He grew weary of the skeptics and the casual thrill seekers. I believe He was probably an introvert. Once caught in a crowd, He couldn't help but spend time with them, because He was moved by compassion on the people (Matt. 9:36; 14:14; 15:32). He could not turn His back on their needs. If He wasn't careful, He would have no time for prayer and for His inner circle.

His motives are fairly clear. He wanted to concentrate on the committed. When Jesus spoke to one crowd, He told them a parable about sowing seed, then said, in effect, "if you get it, you get it." But even His inner circle didn't get it. When they asked Him what He meant, He said, "I speak to them in riddles so you can understand and they can't" (see Matt. 13; Mark 4; Luke 8).

The point is that Jesus' disciples were the good soil—the ones He expected to bring forth a hundredfold—and the crowd were the rocky, weedy soil. And it didn't make sense to keep watering the rocks.

In front of another large crowd (Luke 14:25-33), He said that anyone who wants to follow Him has to hate his or her family—even to the point of giving up the person's spouse (Luke 18:29)—and bear his or her cross. That's how Jesus put hurdles in front of people who wanted to follow Him. "Count the cost," He continued. "It's expensive." He wanted to spend His time with the truly committed; the ones willing to risk everything.

To solve the problem of the crowds Jesus stayed outside the towns in "lonely places" (Mark 1:45, NIV), sending His disciples into town to buy supplies and make preparations, thus giving Him time alone to pray. Notice this tactic in the following verses:

"So he came to a town in Samaria called Sychar, near the plot of ground Jacob had given to his son Joseph. Jacob's well was there, and Jesus, tired as he was from the journey, sat down by the well. It was about noon. . . . (His disciples had gone into the town to buy food.) . . . Then, leaving her water jar, the woman went back to the town and said to the people, 'Come, see a man who told me everything I ever did. Could this be the Messiah?' They came out of the town and made their way toward him" (John 4:5-30, NIV).

"When Martha heard that Jesus was coming, she went out to meet him. . . . And after she had said this, she went back and called her sister Mary aside. 'The Teacher is here,' she said, 'and is asking for you.' When Mary heard this, she got up quickly and went to him. *Now Jesus had not yet entered the village, but was still at the place where Martha had met him*" (John 11:20-30, NIV).

"Then the whole town went out to meet Jesus. And when they saw him, they pleaded with him to leave their region" (Matt 8:34, NIV).

"And he sent messengers on ahead, who went into a Samaritan village to get things ready for him" (Luke 9:52, NIV).

"Jesus sent Peter and John, saying, 'Go and make preparations for us to eat the Passover.' 'Where do you want us to prepare for it?' they asked. He replied, 'As you enter the city, a man carrying a jar of water will meet you. Follow him to the house that he enters' " (Luke 22:8-10, NIV).

"As they approached Jerusalem and came to Bethphage and Bethany at the Mount of Olives, Jesus sent two of his disciples, saying to them, 'Go to the village ahead of you, and just as you enter it, you will find a colt tied there, which no one has ever ridden. Untie it and bring it here' " (Mark 11:1, 2, NIV).

Jesus did not like to go into town—but large cities were even worse. With the exception of Jerusalem, the Holy City, He tended to avoid them entirely.

Perhaps He took seriously Hosea 11:9 LXX: "I am God, and not man; the Holy One within you; and I will not enter into the city."

He probably also shared the opinion of Plato: "I do not know whether philosophy has become something good or bad for me since I now hate to associate with the masses. . . . Therefore I left the city as if it were a cage for animals [cf. Rev. 18:2]. . . . My decision is to be far away from the city, both for the present and as long as God might grant me life."[2]

In addition, He evidently agreed with the Essenes who, according to Philo, "dwell in villages, keeping away from the cities because of lawlessness practiced by city-dwellers. They know that the pestilence bred from this company, as from polluted air, would render their souls incurable."[3] You can see that cities had a bad reputation even then.

But Gentile cities were worse still. They were simply out of the question.

Jesus seems to have had the same scruples as the unnamed Levite in Judges 19:12: "We won't go into any city whose people are not Israelites" (NIV). Although He visited the regions *around* Caesarea Philippi, Gerasa, Decapolis, and Tyre and Sidon, Jesus apparently bypassed the cities themselves. We have no record of any ministry performed by Jesus inside a Gentile city. Separation was His stated policy: "Do not go among the Gentiles or enter any town of the Samaritans" (Matt. 10:5, NIV). Remember, His mission was to the "lost sheep of Israel" (verse 6, NIV; 15:24). So He confined His ministry exclusively to towns of observant, orthodox Jews: Capernaum, Chorazin, Bethsaida, Bethany, Jericho, Gennesaret, Cana, and Nazareth. Scripture has no record of Him entering the larger cities where Hellenized Jews mingled with Gentiles: Hippus, Gadara, Julias (only 100 yards from Bethsaida), Tiberias, Scythopolis, or Caesarea Philippi.

And what was Jesus doing with all this private time in the countryside while the Twelve were away in town? He was in communion with His father.

To list just the passages in Luke: "But Jesus often withdrew to lonely places and prayed" (Luke 5:16, NIV). "Jesus went out to a mountainside to pray, and spent the night praying to God" (Luke 6:12, NIV). "Once when Jesus was praying in private and his disciples were with him, he asked them, 'Who do the crowds say I am?' " (Luke 9:18, NIV). "He took Peter, John and James with him and went up onto a mountain to pray" (Luke 9:28, NIV). "One day Jesus was praying in a certain place. When he finished, one of his disciples said to him, 'Lord, teach us to pray, just as John taught his disciples' " (Luke 11:1, NIV). Even His private teaching came during a prayer break. The main thing was prayer.

Don't you think that the reason Jesus drew the crowds in the first place was because of His alone time? He was a drawing man because He was a withdrawing man. Christ learned that without spending time with God, even He could do nothing. Remember, He started His ministry by spending 40 days alone with the Lord.

Consider the fact that hundreds of sick people died of some illness that Jesus might have healed if only He had worked a little longer instead of sneaking away on a retreat! But He went anyway. First, Jesus fought His battles in the spiritual realm, then He could work effectively in the physical one. Until we learn that, our ministry and our witness will be fruitless.

Nothing is more important. We wrestle not against flesh and blood. Unless we have done our homework in the spiritual realms—unless we strive with God in prayer in advance—we are fighting naked. If we haven't put on the spiritual armor, we're wasting our time.

It is prayer that brings the rain of the Spirit that swells the rivers and floods the soul with glory. Prayer greases the gears of heaven, unleashes heaven's weapons of mass destruction to tear down strongholds of the enemy.

And prayer has lost none of its power to save souls today, as we will see.

---

1. Josephus, *Antiquities of the Jews* 18.118.

2. Abraham J. Malherbe, ed., *The Cynic Epistles* (Missoula, Mont.: Scholars Press/Society of Biblical Literature, 1977), p. 277.

3. Philo, *Quod Omins Probus Liber* 12.76.

**CHAPTER 8**

# Seeking the Lost

Jesus gave us His own personal mission statement in Luke 19:10. It is very simple: to seek and save the lost. I don't see how any church can improve on that.

But any church can enhance the way it goes about it. If we want to see men and women saved in droves, and not trickle in one by one, we have to start with prayer. Not a prayer here and there, but a consistent mass of prayer built up over time. Then the floodgates open, and many lost are saved. Before we can reap them with love and before we can teach them the truth, we have to seek them with prayer.

Great revivals almost always start with prayer. The reason 3,000 joined the Jesus movement on the Day of Pentecost (Acts 2:41) was because the disciples had spent at least 40 days "constantly in prayer" together (Acts 1:14, NIV). It still operates that way today.

Let's look at two great revivals in the United States: one in 1858, and one in 1970. Both of them began with one or two people who decided to pray, and discovered the undiscovered power in the name of Jesus.

In September 1857 the economy of New York City was a shambles. A financial crash had put thousands of merchants out of business. Banks failed, railroads went into bankruptcy, and factories shut down, leaving vast numbers unemployed.

At that time a 46-year-old single businessman by the name of Jeremiah Lanphier, who had a heart for the needy, gave up his business and dedicated his time to lay ministry in the dark slums of Hell's Kitchen. Lanphier poured himself into the lives of people who were homeless, helpless, and hopeless. Month after month he went door to door, distributing tracts and holding Bible studies with whoever would listen.

Then he felt led to start a prayer meeting in the upper room of the consistory building of the North Dutch Reformed Church in Manhattan. He advertised his prayer meeting with 20,000 flyers. On the day appointed, September 23, 1857, he found himself praying alone. After a half hour one other person came up the stairs. By the end of the hour six people had shown up. Hardly an auspicious beginning. But the following week the group grew to 14, then 23. Soon they decided to meet every day for prayer. They filled the Dutch Reformed church, then the Methodist church on John Street, then Trinity Episcopal Church at the corner of Wall Street and Broadway.

By February of 1858 prayer groups crowded every church and every public building in downtown New York, and prayer meetings began to spring up all across America. Horace Greeley, the famous editor, sent a reporter with a horse and buggy racing around to prayer meetings to see how many men were praying. In one hour he could only get to 12 meetings, but he counted 6,100 men.

The revival had little or nothing to do with preaching. People gathered to pray. Sinners came to ask for prayer and were converted on the spot. Parents requested prayer for their unsaved children; and in a few weeks they would receive letters from the children telling of changed lives. For a while 10,000 people a week experienced conversion in New York City. The movement spread throughout New England. Church bells would summon people to prayer at eight in the morning, noon, and six in the evening.

The palpable presence of God seemed to hang over the land, and this canopy of grace even extended out across the Eastern Seaboard. Ships approaching the East Coast began to feel its influence while they were still 100 miles offshore. Vessel after vessel arrived with the passengers telling the same story: a conviction of sin had seized passengers and crew, and they had turned to Christ before reaching port.

During this period churches could not baptize members fast enough. Trinity Episcopal Church in Chicago had 121 members in 1857. By 1860 it had increased to 1,400. Many churches had a similar experience. Between one and two million people were converted to God out of a population of 30 million in one year. The revival jumped the Atlantic and broke out in Northern Ireland, Scotland, Wales, England, South Africa, and south India. It touched Australia on the other side of the planet. The revival began and ended with prayer.

When it reached Chicago, a young shoe salesman went to the Plymouth Congregational Church and asked if he might teach Sunday school. The superintendent said, "I'm sorry, young man, I have 16 teachers too many, but I'll put you on the waiting list."

"I want to do something now," the salesman persisted.

"Well, start a class."

"How do I start a class?"

"Get some boys off the street. Don't bring them here—take them out into the country. After a month you'll have control of them, then bring them here, and that will be your class."

The young man gathered a ragtag group on a beach on Lake Michigan and taught them Bible verses and Bible games. The nicknames of his ragtag converts suggest the kind of people they were: Madden the Butcher, Red Eye, Rag-breeches, Cadet, Black Stove Pipe, Old Man, Darby the Cobbler, Jackie Candles, Smikes, Butcher Lilray, Greenhorn, Indian, Gilberic.

Eventually he took them to the Plymouth Congregational Church. That teacher was Dwight Lyman Moody, and it was the beginning of a 40-year ministry.

Moody's Sunday School class grew so large that president-elect Abraham Lincoln came to visit it.

Now let's skip a few years and look at one incident from the later life of D. L. Moody as told by E. M. Bounds. Moody was taking a sabbatical in London for several months while his new church was under construction in Chicago. He had determined not to do any speaking, but one pastor prevailed upon him to talk to his church. After he preached that Sunday morning, Moody greatly regretted having promised to preach also that night. Later he said he had never had such a hard time preaching anywhere in his life. The church was absolutely cold and dead, without a trace of the moving of God's Spirit.

That evening, however, everything was different. The church was packed, and the place was warm and alive with the Spirit. "The powers of an unseen world seem to have fallen upon the audience," Moody said. He felt impressed to make an altar call, contrary to his plans, and 500 came forward. Thinking they had misunderstood, he sent them back to their seats, told them to count the cost of their decision, then made the call again. The same group came forward again. A major revival started in that church and that neighborhood. Hundreds of lives changed.

What made the difference that night? It turned out that one of the church members had gone home from the morning service to where she lived with an invalid sister who could not get out to the service. When she told her sister that they had a visiting speaker by the name of Dwight Moody, the old woman turned pale. "I read about him some time ago in an American paper, and I have been praying to God to send him to London, and to our church. If I had known he was going to preach this morning, I would have eaten no breakfast. I would have spent the whole time he was preaching in prayer for him. Now, sister, go out of the room, lock the door, send me no dinner, and no matter who comes, don't let them see me. I am going to spend the whole afternoon and evening in prayer."

And that was the secret of Moody's success in London. Someone had prayed to break the ice.

Dwight L. Moody was instrumental in changing the life of F. B. Meyer, who helped to revive a discouraged Wilbur Chapman, who was instrumental in launching the evangelistic career of Billy Sunday. The preaching of Billy Sunday brought transformation to a young man named J. L. Shuler, who later became a powerful evangelist in the Seventh-day Adventist Church. Another person influenced by Sunday was a man by the name of Mordecai Ham, and he in turn brought to the faith a young fellow by the name of Billy Graham. And so the story goes on. A great avalanche of divine power began with the dedication to prayer on the part of one Jeremiah Lanphier.

\* \* \*

In Luke 11:5-13 Jesus explained how persevering prayer unlocks the windows of heaven so that God's Spirit can flow down in great cataracts:

> Then Jesus said to them, "Suppose you have a friend, and you go to him at midnight and say, 'Friend, lend me three loaves of bread; a friend of mine on a journey has come to me, and I have no food to offer him.' And suppose the one inside answers, 'Don't bother me. The door is already locked, and my children and I are in bed. I can't get up and give you anything.' I tell you, even though he will not get up and give you the bread because of friendship, yet because of your shameless audacity he will surely get up and give you as much as you need.
>
> "So I say to you: Ask and it will be given to you; seek and you will find; knock and the door will be opened to you. For everyone who asks receives; the one who seeks finds; and to the one who knocks, the door will be opened.
>
> "Which of you fathers, if your son asks for a fish, will give him a snake instead? Or if he asks for an egg, will give him a scorpion? If you then, though you are evil, know how to give good gifts to your children, how much more will your Father in heaven give the Holy Spirit to those who ask him!" (NIV).

More than 100 years after Jeremiah Lanphier God empowered a handful of teenagers to start another spiritual avalanche through persevering prayer.

In October 1969 six students at Asbury College in Wilmore, Kentucky, covenanted together to conduct what they called the Great Experiment for 30 days. They pledged to spend 30 minutes each morning in prayer with the Word, writing down what truth they got from Scripture. They also pledged to share their faith with someone that day, and to meet once a week to check up on each other.

At the beginning of the winter term each one of those six picked five other people and formed a new group, so now there were six groups of six. That experiment ran for 30 days and ended January 30, 1970. On January 31 those 36 students held the chapel service in the school's Hughes Auditorium. All 36 of them sat on the stage. In that very moving chapel service they stood one by one and told about their experience and what God had done for them. Then they challenged every student in the student body to commit themselves to become part of a group of six and to sign a printed commitment card to that effect.

At the same time, one young student had become deeply concerned that fall for the need of the blessing of God on the campus. She gathered a small group of students around her to pray. Eventually they started having all-night prayer meetings. They prayed for God to come. When they finished their prayer meeting, they would look at each other and ask, "Do you think He'll come today?" The last all-night meeting they had, on February 2, 1970, ended early, at two-thirty in the morning, because they were suddenly impressed at that time that they had prayed enough. They did not need any more prayer. God would come tomorrow. So they returned home and went to bed.

The next day at the chapel service on February 3, God showed up, and all heaven broke loose.

Asbury is a Wesleyan institution that had experienced major revivals in 1905, 1907, 1908, 1915, 1921, 1950, and 1958. Inscribed on the cornerstone of the campus church in which the revival began is a quotation from Hebrews 12:14: "Without holiness, no one will see the Lord."

On Monday morning, February 3, the students assembled in the campus church. Since they had no scheduled speaker, and the new president of the college, Dennis Kinlaw, was traveling, Custer Reynolds, Asbury's academic dean, was in charge. Reynolds did not preach. Instead, he briefly gave his testimony, then issued an invitation for students to talk about their own Christian experiences. After a moment two or three stepped forward, and one of them began to speak.

Suddenly a powerful conviction settled upon the entire congregation, and students began streaming to the front. Others outside the church found themselves spontaneously drawn inside. They forgot lunch in favor of confession of sin, reconciliation of enemies, and praise to the Lord.

There was no leader. Someone asked Dr. Kinlaw to return home, but when he finally arrived at the meeting the next day, he sat down in the back corner, realizing that the Holy Spirit was in charge, and he had better not interfere. Without any sort of leadership, that revival continued round the clock. The service had been scheduled for 50 minutes. Instead, it lasted 185 hours nonstop, 24 hours a day. It continued intermittently for weeks. Ultimately, it spread across the United States and into foreign countries.

From the Asbury campus hundreds of students traveled all over the United States, bringing the revival to more than 200 other colleges. Dennis Kinlaw explains what happened when they told their story in his book *Preaching in the Spirit:*

> Dr. Donald Irwin, pastor of the college church at Olivet Nazarene College in Kankakee, Illinois, was preparing to enter the Saturday night service of a weekend revival when his head usher told him two students from Asbury College wanted to see him. Noting that he still had ten minutes before the service was to begin, Dr. Irwin told the usher he could bring them in.
>
> Two very ordinary-looking young men strode into his study. They told the pastor that revival had broken out at Asbury, that many people who had never known God were finding Him, and that Christians were finding Him in a more powerful way. These two fellows had been praying together the night before, when God told them they should visit Olivet College and share with the students what God was doing at Asbury.
>
> Dr. Irwin expressed his delight at the news, but indicated that he could not invite them to speak from the pulpit of the church because they were strangers to him. Their response surprised him. They said, "No problem! God told us to come. We've obeyed Him. So everything's fine." Dr. Irwin sensed no negative feelings on their part as he turned them away and they started down the hall.
>
> Dr. Irwin's own spirit checked him. He found himself calling, "Wait a minute, fellows. Come back. How long will it take you to share your story? Could you do it in five minutes, after the first hymn?"
>
> They assured him they could do it in less time, if he desired. They just wanted to be obedient to the Holy Spirit.

So after the opening hymn, Dr. Irwin briefly introduced the two students. The first stood and simply told who he was and how God was at work in Asbury College. He indicated that many people were finding God, torn relationships were being repaired, lives were being transformed, and the Lord had told them to come and share the news. He sat down and the second student arose and said about the same thing. The two young men took no more than four minutes to tell their story and there was no noticeable response from the crowd. Dr. Irwin announced that a quartet would sing next.

The quartet finished their first verse. Before they could begin the second, their bass went to the altar, sobbing. Twelve to fifteen other people rose from various places in the auditorium and came to the altar.

The service was being broadcast by radio. Many who listened felt the tug of God at their hearts, left what they were doing, and drove to the church. By nine o'clock there were more people in the sanctuary than when the service began. Many who came did not stop to take a seat but went directly to the altar to make their peace with God.

The next morning, about twenty carloads of students drove from Olivet to churches and colleges around the country to tell about the revival. Wherever they went, the Spirit attended their witness as He had that of the two students the night before.[1]

Scores of Asbury students had similar experiences. It seemed that the less outgoing the students were—the more shy—the more lives they touched. The Holy Spirit just needed a channel to work through.

* * *

Now skip down to the fall of 1970. I don't know if there was a direct connection between what happened at Asbury that winter and what happened at Andrews University, or whether the Spirit of God was just flowing at flood level that year.

That particular year Andrews was seething with dissidence, drug abuse, and racial polarization. Hairstyles and dress were divisive issues on campus. The raucous crows of the 1960s had come to roost at Andrews.

Certain members of the faculty and a group of students began to pray for revival at the school. Before classes started, they laid plans to have a fall Campus Concern Retreat at Camp Michiana involving the student leaders and others. The students who came had already been studying and praying together for a year or more, which puts them in the same time frame as the small groups at Asbury. These youth had dedicated themselves to changing the spiritual status quo.

Guest speakers for the retreat were E. L. Minchin, H. M. S. Richards, Jr., and a 29-year-old pastor by the name of Mike Stevenson. Stevenson was convinced that formalism, not fanaticism, was the problem in the Seventh-day Adventist Church.

What happened next illustrates a theme that runs through revival literature: revival is more frequently sparked by testimony—often lay testimony—than by expository preaching (though we certainly need more of that). God calls men and women to be witnesses, not orators—channels of grace, not chalices of wisdom.

During the preliminary hymn at one of the main evening meetings, Stevenson felt deeply impressed that something out of the ordinary was about to happen, so he excused himself and went to his cabin to pray. When he came back, he had left his sermon notes behind and simply gave his personal testimony of what God had done in his life.

The result was an avalanche. The students began praying and confessing their sins at 9:00 and did not stop until 3:00 A.M. At one point they moved to a campfire and broke up into small groups and began to pray that the Lord would awaken those who had already gone to sleep, and many of them actually stirred from a sound sleep, came to the campfire, and gave their hearts to Christ.

That was the beginning of something big.

When 150 revived students returned to campus, they encountered skepticism and ridicule. But on Tuesday, at a 9:00 chapel, when they stood before the student body and told what God had done for them, it electrified the campus. The students invited their friends to give their lives to Christ. Chapel didn't let out until noon, and the school suspended classes that day. From there the revival just kept growing. It produced all-night prayer meetings, chapel testimony services, and singing in the cafeteria food line.

The campus became polarized—some of the faculty were against the revival, others for it. But the revival went forward, and hundreds of lives definitely changed. The students had a bonfire at which they burned their drug paraphernalia, rock music, and pornography. The wind of God blew through the campus and cleansed it.

Immediately the Holy Spirit transformed the students into missionaries. Teams of youth went out to all the nearby academies and churches. According to the *Student Movement* of December 3, 1970, 18 university students left the campus to carry the revival to Columbia Union College (CUC). The service at Sligo Church, on the campus there, ran until 2:30 P.M. after an all-night Friday evening service.

Next, carloads of students from CUC traveled at their own expense to surrounding churches to share the revival. Soon they hit Southern Missionary College (now Southern Adventist University), where 500 students volunteered to prepare a special Bible-in-the-hand witnessing program.

It was about that time that I went forward for a moving call during the Week of Prayer held at Collegedale Academy, dedicated myself to God, and volunteered to join a seminar group that visited small churches in the area to hold services. I didn't know it, but that was my summons to the ministry. I had no inkling at the time of any connection to Andrews University, or even to Southern. I just know I felt the leading of God.

During the next several years the spark that had ignited in the hearts of those Andrews students burst into flame and spread to many of the major Adventist colleges around the world.

Tens of thousands of people found salvation in the 1970 revivals that started at Asbury. Millions of lives were touched all because one young woman decided to pray. The prayers of that handful of young Christians unleashed a tornado of holy power that swept across the nation.

It was the last great revival to sweep America. Will there ever be another? Or has America's time of grace passed?

Saving the lost can be a complicated business, just like raising a crop. God does the growing, but we do the fertilizing, weeding, and harvesting. Saving the lost requires prayer, love, and truth. People need to be prayed for, loved into fellowship, and established in the truth.

There are precise techniques for dealing with human souls. These are important. But technique is nothing without dedicated prayer. Prayer changes the world. Stay tuned.

---

1. Dennis F. Kinlaw, *Preaching in the Spirit* (Wilmore, Ky.: Francis Asbury Press, 1985), pp. 102, 103.

# CHAPTER 9

# Money and the Christian

Jesus had more to say about money than almost any other subject. And He says more about it in Luke than anywhere else. But few Christians have ever read what He said very carefully. They think He taught that Christians should be generous toward everyone and perhaps tithe their income. But Jesus was much more radical than that!

In this chapter we will see that the original apostles didn't give a mere 10 percent of their income to the cause, they gave 100 percent. Literally. That is why the New Testament has so little to say about tithing. The Twelve had nothing to tithe since after they became disciples they had no money, no jobs, and no income. Furthermore, Christianity had not yet broken from Judaism. They were a sect of Judaism known as "the Way." As long as the Temple continued to stand, the earliest Christian leaders did not appropriate to themselves the tithe, which belonged to the Temple. Local freewill offerings took care of their daily needs.

Even before Jesus, John the Baptist had called his disciples to share their goods. " 'The ax is already at the root of the trees, and every tree that does not produce good fruit will be cut down and thrown into the fire.' 'What should we do then?' the crowd asked. John answered, 'Anyone who has two shirts should share with the one who has none, and anyone who has food should do the same' " (Luke 3:9-11, NIV). The kingdom is about to come, so give away your extra stuff to those who have less.

Jesus took up John's theme and made it more radical. He told His disciples to "sell your possessions and give to the poor" while they were "waiting for their master to return from a wedding banquet" (Luke 12:33, 36, NIV). Note the full context of the passage: do not worry about food and clothing (verses 22-31), distribute possessions to the needy (verses 32-34), and be ready for the Master to return unexpectedly (verses 35-40).

Does that remind you of anything? That's the counsel the Millerites followed as they awaited what they thought was the coming of Jesus in 1844. Our spiritual forebears took Jesus very seriously, and did *exactly what He said to do.*

Jesus told all His listeners—not just the rich young ruler—to sell everything and give to the poor. He said, "As for what is inside you—be generous to the poor, and everything will be clean for you" (Luke 11:41, NIV). "Sell your possessions and give to the poor. Provide purses for yourselves that will not wear out, a treasure in heaven that will never fail, where no thief comes near and no moth destroys" (Luke 12:33, NIV). "Those of you who do not give up everything you have cannot be my disciples" (Luke 14:33, NIV).

The 12 apostles took Him seriously. We discover this when we analyze Mark's account of the promising young man Jesus wanted for a disciple. Mark 10:21 says that Jesus fell in love with his earnestness. " 'One thing you lack,' he said. 'Go, sell everything you have and give to the poor, and you will have treasure in heaven. Then come, follow me' " (NIV).

That young man went away sad, holding his wealth close to his heart, when he could have exchanged it for riches greater than he could imagine.

We always stop reading at this point, but what follows is very interesting. "Then Peter spoke up, 'We *have* left everything to follow you!' " (verse 28, NIV). The point is that the rest of the disciples *had already done what Jesus asked the rich young ruler to do.*

Modern Christians comfort themselves with the idea that what Jesus requested of the rich young ruler was a special case. No Christian wants to be burdened with such a stringent requirement for discipleship today. But the traditional Jesus we have tailored to fit comfortably into our world is wishful thinking. It is only another example of the eternal desire of everyone, of all persuasions, to reduce the strangeness of Jesus and see Him as someone who, well, believes what they were taught to believe.

Mea culpa. I used to say that Jesus could not have meant His advice to sell all of one's goods as applying to everyone because those who turned over all their goods to the poor would, of course, themselves become poor, requiring the support of others, which only transfers the poverty. But this apparently intractable problem begins to yield when we stop thinking like Western individualists and instead like . . . well, communists (or, if it makes you feel better, communalists). As long as the community keeps growing, the influx of new members continually enlarges the communal kitty. First, we join and give our all to support others, then newer converts turn over their goods to support us—a system not all that different, come to think of it, from our modern system of Social Security or life insurance, just more radical.

In fact, come to think of it, all organized groups, religions, corporations, and even nations are, in effect, pyramid schemes that depend on a constant influx of new members, workers, customers, soldiers, taxpayers, citizens. It is for this reason that the ultimate economic threat is low birth rates. And low birth rates result from—now this is totally counterintuitive—a culture that encourages sexual immorality. That's right. Caesar Augustus discovered this before the birth of Christ and passed his Julian laws to counteract it. Modern pundits, however, are clueless. And that is, I believe, the main reason for the ongoing collapse of Western civilization. Intriguing, isn't it? I have much more to say about this, but you cannot bear it now. That will take another book.

And now, back to our regularly scheduled discussion of Mark 10.

Following Peter's statement "We have left everything to follow you," in Mark 10:28 we find a very extravagant promise that Jesus made to those who, like the apostles, give up everything for the kingdom. He promised that they would acquire *in this life* 100 times as many houses, brothers, sisters, mothers, and fields, and later, in the age to come, eternal life (verse 30). That was the boon that Jesus was offering the rich young ruler if only he had been able to see with the eyes of faith.

What? Say that again? *This* life?

At first glance such a promise sounds like pie-in-the-sky nonsense. Why would Jesus, who denounced mammon (Luke 16:9, 11, 13), entice His disciples with houses and lands in the first place? How could the same person who said, "Those of you who do not give up everything you have cannot be my disciples" (Luke 14:33, NIV) turn around and promise 100 times as many houses and lands *in the here and now*? Stop and think about it before you go on. Exercise your mental muscles. It's good for you. Sleep on it, maybe.

The question provides its own answer. Once we surrender private possessions, then everything belongs to everyone, who now have 100 times as much.

Jesus said something that sheds light on His way of thinking. Recall that when His mother and brothers came looking for Him, He claimed that His *real* mothers and brothers were those who did God's will (Mark 3:32-35; Matt. 12:46-50; Luke 8:20, 21). So already He had 100 mothers and brothers. And when, in Mark 10:30, He called for outsiders to multiply their mothers and brothers and fields *in this life* by joining the movement, He was only offering them what He already enjoyed.

What Jesus demanded of the rich young ruler, then, was no more than what He required of all His disciples—or at least all those who, like the rich *young* (Matt. 19:20) ruler, were young and teachable enough to be invited into His inner circle.

Luke is not the only source for the idea that Jesus asked the early disciples to give all. We see hints of it in the other Gospels, such as the two short parables in Matthew 13:44-46 about a man who "sold all he had" (the phrase common to both parables) to secure the kingdom: "The kingdom of heaven is like treasure hidden in a field. When a man found it, he hid it again, and then in his joy went and *sold all he had* and bought that field. Again, the kingdom of heaven is like a merchant looking for fine pearls. When he found one of great value, he went away and *sold everything he had* and bought it" (NIV).

Then there is the cry of "some" in the group around Jesus that the perfume poured on Him by the woman who washed His feet with her hair "could have been sold for more than a year's wages and the money given to the poor" (Mark 14:5, NIV). This is nothing more than a restatement of the rule given by Jesus Himself in Luke 11:41 and 12:33, overzealously applied at the wrong time to the wrong person.

But the other Gospels lack most of Jesus' teaching about giving possessions to the poor found in Luke 6:20; 11:41; 12:33; 18:22; 19:8. Only Jesus' words to the rich young ruler have a close parallel in the other Gospels (Mark 10:21; Matt. 19:21; Luke 18:22). This suggests to me that Luke abandoned his medical career as the disciples did their nets, and conferred his goods on the poor like all the Jerusalem disciples (Acts 2:44-46). Jesus' teaching validated Luke's personal experience, and he felt strongly about it.

Although mainline Judaism of Jesus' day said little about giving up one's possessions, the prophets did teach that on the day of the Lord God's people would have to discard their material possessions (Prov. 1:4; Isa. 2:20; 24:2; Ezek. 7:12, 13, 19; Zeph. 1:18; cf. Matt. 24:17, 18). Why not dispose of them now, Jesus taught, and lay up treasure in heaven? After all, the kingdom is at hand.

Not every early Christian sold everything *immediately*. A large fortune takes awhile to get rid of. Even in Jerusalem the believers at first broke bread "in their homes" (Acts 2:46, NIV). Yet they seem to have regarded those homes not as private property but as open to all believers, held in common until they could be sold. But soon after Pentecost the followers of "the Way" fulfilled Jesus' command to "sell your possessions and give to the poor" (Matt. 19:21; Luke 12:33, NIV), just as the Twelve had before the Crucifixion: "All the believers were together and had everything in common. They sold property and possessions to give to anyone who had need" (Acts 2:44, 45, NIV).

"All the believers were one in heart and mind. No one claimed that any of their possessions was their own, but they shared everything they had. . . . There were no needy persons among them. For from time to time those who owned land or houses sold them, brought the money from the sales and put it at the apostles' feet, and it was distributed to anyone who had need" (Acts 4:32-35, NIV).

The "everything in common" rule did not suddenly spring up after the Resurrection. The earliest Christian communities were only imitating the original practice of the Twelve. The original commune of the Twelve had now grown large.

It seems that one individual, though, tried to cheat the system. When Ananias sold some land and donated only part of the proceeds, Peter rebuked him: "Ananias, how is it that Satan has so filled your heart that you have lied to the Holy Spirit and have kept for yourself some of the money you received for the land? Didn't it belong to you before it was sold? And after it was sold, wasn't the money at your disposal? What made you think of doing such a thing? You have not lied just to human beings but to God" (Acts 5:3, 4, NIV).

People usually cite Peter's question, "Wasn't the money at your disposal?" as evidence that not all believers were required to offer up all of their property. Maybe. On the other hand, it may mean only that the property had no lien-holders or co-owners, so the proceeds were wholly under their control. We routinely ignore the context of this story because of the chapter break. But the context (Acts 4:32-37) suggests that what was expected of Barnabas and the other believers—"*no one* claimed . . . *any of their possessions*"—was also expected of Ananias and Sapphira. Otherwise, why should they not be free to give as much as they pleased at any point in the process? The story mentions no special, individual pledge; rather, it is the common pledge expected of the entire group that the couple violated.

Frankly—there is no easy way to say it—the first Christians were communists! Theistic communists, of course—Jesus was no Marxist. He did not reject the principles of capitalism. The parable of the minas in Luke 19:11-26 clearly assumes capitalistic values. (We will discuss the horrors of modern Marxist Communism shortly.)

At any rate, the early Christian movement was clearly dedicated to equality in a way that modern Communism aspires to but never reaches, since its leaders do not set an example but live large at the expense of the proletariat (the middle class). Christianity teaches that "you are all one" (Gal. 3:28, NIV; 1 Cor. 12:20-27; 2 Cor. 8:13-15), and is dedicated to *koinonia*. This New Testament word is most interesting. Christian tradition usually translates it as "fellowship," but as we will see it is in fact Plato's technical term for the practice of communism.

The Greek root *koinos* ("common") and its cognates (related words drawn from the same Greek root) have a similar range of meaning as the English cognates "commune, communal, communism, community"—that is, "common unity," all one, all things in common.[1] *Koinonia* connotes a community that practices "share and share alike." The root *koin* occurs in verb form in the following verses: "*Share* with God's people who are in need" (Rom. 12:13, NIV); "For if the Gentiles have *shared* in the Jews' spiritual blessings, they owe it to the Jews to *share* with them their material blessings" (Rom. 15:27, NIV); "They urgently pleaded with us for the privilege of *sharing* in this service to the saints" (2 Cor. 8:4, NIV); "Men will praise God . . . for your generosity in *sharing* with them and with everyone else" (2 Cor. 9:13, NIV); and in many other verses.

* * *

Jesus and the disciples were by no means the first to hold all things in common. Remember that Jesus grew up in "Galilee of the Gentiles" (Matt. 4:15, NIV; Isa. 9:1). The main influence on His life was the Hebrew Scriptures. However, unlike Judea, "Galilee of the Gentiles" was a cosmopolitan environment where He might have tapped into Greek ideals.

The communist group that Jesus would have known best would have been the nearby Essenes, who also called their doctrine "the Way," just like the early Christians (Acts 9:2; 19:9, 23; 22:4; 24:5, 14, 22; 28:22).[2] The Essenes despised riches, held all things in common, and carried no luggage on their journeys except a defensive weapon, knowing that they always had a place to stay with a fellow Essene in any city to which they might travel.[3]

"You will not find one among them [anyone] distinguished by greater opulence than another. They have a law that new members on admission to the sect shall confiscate their property to the order, with the result that you will nowhere see either abject poverty or inordinate wealth; the individual's possessions join the community stock and all, like brothers, enjoy a single patrimony. . . . They elect officers [Acts 6:1-7] to attend to the interests of the community, the special services of each officer being determined by the whole body."[4]

Contemporary Essene practice may shed some light on the story of Ananias and Sapphira. The Dead Sea scroll 1QS, called *The Rule of the Community* (formerly called *The Manual of Discipline*), requires all who wish to join the Essene community to offer up all their possessions: "All those who freely devote themselves to His truth shall bring all their knowledge, powers, and possessions into the Community of God, that they may purify their knowledge in the truth of God's precepts, and order their powers according to His ways of perfection, and all their possessions according to His righteous counsel." But some novitiates felt tempted to withhold something on the side. "These are the rules by which they shall judge at a Community (court of) inquiry according to the cases: If one of them has lied deliberately in matters of property, he shall be excluded from the pure Meal of the Congregation for one year and shall do penance with respect to one quarter of his food."[5]

Ananias and Sapphira met with a more severe fate. Perhaps their only sin was lying about the amount for which they had sold the land (Acts 5:3, 4, 8). At any rate, the penalty was sudden death—harsh, perhaps, but not as much as the larger number who died under the curses of Elijah and Elisha in 2 Kings 1:9-15; 2:24. The outcome was that "great fear" fell upon the believers (Acts 5:11). Sometimes at the beginning of new movements, God has to set an example with those who toy around with Him. A little fear now prevents a lot of suffering later.

According to Josephus, the Essenes "live the same kind of life as do those whom the Greeks call Pythagoreans."[6] His statement linking the Essenes to the philosophical tradition begun by Pythagoras opens to us new vistas on the life of Jesus, because Pythagoras also had a group of disciples who also practiced vegetarianism and communism.

Communism began with Pythagoras (ca. 569-ca. 480 B.C.), who influenced Socrates (ca. 469-399 B.C.), whose disciple was Plato (428-348 B.C.), whose disciple was Aristotle (384-322 B.C.), whose disciple was Alexander the Great, who spread Aristotle's philosophy around the world.

Another disciple of Socrates was Antisthenes (ca. 445-ca. 365 B.C.), whose disciple was Diogenes (412?-323 B.C.). Antisthenes and Diogenes founded the Cynics. The Cynics of Jesus' day were wandering, long-haired philosophers who wore a tattered, bare-shouldered garment; carried a wallet and staff; didn't marry or build homes; rejected societal norms and reviled convention; and despised wealth and proclaimed the gospel of simplicity. They lived off the donations of others. They were the hippies of ancient times.

A center of Cynic philosophy existed at Gadara, only 20 miles from Nazareth—much closer than Jerusalem—from which Cynic preachers went out to spread the message. Jesus probably listened to many a wandering, long-haired Cynic philosopher during His first 30 years.

All of these ideas trace back to Pythagoras, whom most people today know as discoverer of the mathematical rule that the square of the hypotenuse equals the squares of the two sides of a triangle. But Pythagoras was much more than a mathematician; he was a moral reformer who taught his disciples to despise wealth. According to Diogenes Laertius, "Pythagoras was the first person who invented the term philosophy, and who called himself a philosopher." "He was the first person, as Timaeus says, who asserted that the property of friends is common, and that friendship is equality. And his disciples used to put all their possessions together into one store, and use them in common."[7] So Pythagoras, the first philosopher, was also the first communist.

As we have seen, the philosophy of Pythagoras was adopted by Socrates, who lived simply, disdaining creature comforts. He allegedly said, "There is perhaps nothing unusual about some people inquiring, first of all, why I have chosen a life of poverty while others zealously pursue wealth, and then why, although it is possible for me to get large sums of money from many people, I willingly refuse gifts not only from living friends, but also from friends who have died and left gifts to me. . . . I am satisfied to have the plainest food and the same garment summer and winter, and I do not wear shoes at all, nor do I desire political fame."[8]

When put on trial for "corrupting the youth," Socrates said in his defense, according to Plato's *Apology*, something that sounds suspiciously like several passages of Scripture:

> Men of Athens, I honor and love you; but I shall obey God rather than you [compare Acts 4:18-20; 5:27-29], and while I have life and strength I shall never cease from the practice and teaching of philosophy, exhorting anyone whom I meet after my manner, and convincing him, saying: O my friend, why do you who are a citizen of the great and mighty and wise city of Athens, care so much about laying up the greatest amount of money and honor and reputation, and so little about wisdom and truth and the greatest improvement of the soul, which you never regard or heed at all? [compare Luke 12:15-21]. . . .
>
> For I do nothing but go about persuading you all, old and young alike, not to take thought for your persons and your properties, but first and chiefly to care about the greatest improvement of the soul [compare Matt. 6:24-34]. I tell you that virtue is not given by money, but that from virtue come money and every other good of man, public as well as private. This is my teaching, and if this is the doctrine which corrupts the youth, my influence is ruinous indeed.

In spite of his defense, Socrates, like Jesus, was condemned to death. But his ideas lived on in the writings of his disciple Aristotle. "The proverb 'what friends have is common property' expresses the truth," he writes, "for friendship depends on community [communism (*koinonia*)]." "Among ourselves, whatever may be the number of citizens, the property is always distributed among them, and therefore no one is in want." "As to common meals, there is a general agreement that a well ordered city should have them . . . open to all the citizens."[9]

*The Cynic Epistles* show that after the death of Socrates his disciples shared their goods. For example, Aeschines provides for Xanthippe (epistle 21), and the writer of epistle 26 urges Plato to write and ask for anything needed, as "my possessions, Plato, are by all rights yours, even as they were Socrates."[10]

Plato holds up communism (*koinonia*) as a shining hope, giving us what almost sounds like a recipe for the earliest Christian community in Jerusalem:

> The first and highest form of the state and of the government and of the law is that in which there prevails most widely the ancient saying, that "Friends have all things in common." Whether there is anywhere now, or will ever be, this communion of women and children and of property, in which the private and individual is altogether banished from life, . . . whether all this is possible or not, I say that no man, acting upon any other principle, will ever constitute a state which will be truer or better or more exalted in virtue. Whether such a state is governed by gods or sons of gods, one, or more than one, happy are the men who, living after this manner, dwell there; and therefore to this we are to look for the pattern of the state, and to cling to this, and to seek with all our might for one which is like this. . . . Let the citizens at once distribute their land and houses.[11]

Plato's dream of a communistic society came largely true early in the book of Acts, though it did not include the sharing of wives and children.

However, Christian communism did not work out so well in the long run. Communism usually fails eventually, no matter how virtuous its practitioners. Perhaps the Jerusalem community failed because the new kingdom Jesus was setting up was never intended to be a lengthy holding operation in a faithless world, but a universal family of faith under God, something like the egalitarian utopia described in the *Sibylline Oracles,* a Jewish document written around the time Jesus was born:

"The earth will belong equally to all, undivided by walls or fences. It will then bear more abundant fruits spontaneously. Lives will be in common and wealth will have no division. For there will be no poor man there, no rich, and no tyrant, no slave. Further, no one will be either great or small anymore. No kings, no leaders. All will be on a par together."[12]

Unfortunately, such a utopian philosophy did not fit well the circumstances of the old age of sin. All too soon trouble entered paradise. Tensions developed between the Hebrews and the Hellenists over the public dole of food (Acts 6:1). Even more serious problems developed at Thessalonica.

Many idealistic societies start out by practicing "all things in common." The American colonists tried it—devout Christians, most of them—but abandoned it before they all starved. It's an instructive tale, worthy of retelling.

The early European settlers of Roanoke, Jamestown, and Plymouth practiced forms of communism. The fields were communally owned, and all toiled together for the common good. As a result, many of the settlers starved to death.

Finally, in desperation, the Pilgrims broke up the land trust, parceling it out to individual owners, and the harvest grew bounteous. Plymouth governor William Bradford, an eyewitness, described the changeover in his *History of Plymouth Plantation*, written ca. 1650:

> They began to think how they might raise as much corn as they could, and obtain a better crop than they had done, that they might not still thus languish in misery. At length, after much debate of things, the Governor (with the advice of the chiefest amongst them) gave way that they should set corn every man for his own particular, and in that regard trust to themselves; in all other thing to go on in the general way as before. And so assigned to every family a parcel of land, according to the proportion of their number for that end, only for present use (but made no division for inheritance) and ranged all boys and youth under some family. This had very good success, for it made all hands very industrious, so as much more corn was planted than otherwise would have been by any means the Governor or any other could use, and saved him a great deal of trouble, and gave far better content. The women now went willingly into the field, and took their little ones with them to set corn; which before would allege weakness and inability; whom to have compelled would have been thought great tyranny and oppression.
>
> The experience that was had in this common course and condition, tried sundry years, and that amongst godly and sober men, may

well evince the vanity of that conceit of Plato and other ancients, applauded by some of later times; and that the taking away of property and bringing in community into a commonwealth would make them happy and flourishing; as if they were wiser than God. For this community (so far as it was) was found to breed much confusion and discontent, and retard much employment that would have been to their benefit and comfort. For the young men that were most able and fit for labor and service did repine that they should spend their time and strength to work for other men's wives and children without any recompense. The strong, or man of parts, had no more in division of victuals and clothes than he that was weak and not able to do a quarter the other could; this was thought injustice. The aged and graver men to be ranked and equalized in labors and victuals, clothes, etc., with the meaner and younger sort, thought it some indignity and disrespect unto them. And for men's wives to be commanded to do service for other men, as dressing their meat, washing their clothes, etc., they deemed it a kind of slavery, neither could many husbands well brook it. Upon the point all being to have alike, and all to do alike, they thought themselves in the like condition, and one as good as another; and so, if it did not cut off those relations that God hath set amongst men, yet it did at least much diminish and take off the mutual respects that should be preserved amongst them. And would have been worse if they had been men of another condition. Let none object this is men's corruption, and nothing to the course itself. I answer, seeing all men have this corruption in them, God in His wisdom saw another course fitter for them.

The Plymouth Colony fiasco illustrates the problem with communism almost everywhere: the lazy members of the community take advantage of the more industrious.

All of this history helps us understand the difficulties Paul encountered among his own converts in the middle of the first century. The persecution of A.D. 34 (Acts 8:1) had scattered the believers and their lifestyle abroad. About 18 years later Paul composed the Thessalonian Epistles, often regarded as the first documents of the New Testament ever written. In Thessalonians we find an interesting dynamic between the Christians who were living off the land, so to speak, and those who worked for a living. Those groups who refused to work were either a holdover from the earliest Christian community in Jerusalem or else, like the Millerite movement, a replay of it. They thought Jesus was about to come. Why work?

So Paul encouraged the believers in Thessalonica to work with their hands and be independent (1 Thess. 4:11) and to warn those who were still idle (1 Thess. 5:14).

It is no mere coincidence that right in between these two injunctions is another passage (1 Thess. 4:13-5:11) discussing the Second Coming, in which Paul answers questions about the fate of those believers who, contrary to expectations, had already died before Jesus' return.

The reason that we find the two subjects—the imminence of the Second Coming and work and idleness—juxtaposed in 1 Thessalonians 4 is because they are related as cause (Jesus is coming soon) and effect (no need to concern oneself with earthly affairs). After all, had not Jesus ordered His disciples not to worry about food and clothing or make any plans for tomorrow (Matt. 6:31-34; Luke 12:29-33)? The idlers no doubt felt that they were imitating the apostles and living by faith, following the dictates of the Sermon on the Mount.

By the time the apostle wrote 2 Thessalonians a few months later, the shirkers were still a serious problem. Paul's remedy was to point out that the Second Coming was not quite so near as some thought (2 Thess. 2:3). A few things had to happen first. The no-labor faction would never go back to work as long as they believed Jesus might return any day now. At this point the Christian community had to ostracize the idle (2 Thess. 3:6-15). No work, wrote Paul, no eat. Their behavior had become dysfunctional and fanatical. Paul must have sensed that the long-term viability of the community depended upon some means of producing wealth (e.g., tentmaking, Acts 18:3). So he offered no support for the "do no work and live off the generosity of others" philosophy. Even if that was the apostolic ideal, it didn't work well as a rule for everyone in the Gentile communities that Paul ministered to. Thus in Thessalonians you might say that Paul found it necessary to modify the teaching of Jesus—or at least to clarify that what applied to the apostles did not always apply to the laity.

Notice how things had changed in the 20 years since Pentecost. At first "there were no needy persons among them" (Acts 4:34, NIV). Later, though, Paul had to solicit contributions "for the poor among the Lord's people in Jerusalem" (Rom. 15:26, NIV; cf. Gal. 2:10), finally returning "to Jerusalem to bring my people gifts for the poor" (Acts 24:17, NIV). The poor, it seems, are always with us.

So early Christian communism was hardly an unqualified success. The fact that even the fervent, idealistic, self-sacrificing community of Acts failed within 20 years bodes poorly for the long-term viability of any sort of communism. Regardless of the philosophy behind it, whether theistic or atheistic, pure communism *just doesn't work*. It's contrary to human nature, since only a few of the most ardent believers will work harder to improve common property than to enhance their own. It is a well-established fact that nations begin to prosper once they enact laws to protect private ownership of property.

The collapse of Christian communism in Jerusalem was not the end of it in Christianity. About the end of the first century a very important Christian document, the Didache, prescribed: "You shall not turn away from someone in need, but shall share everything with your brother, and not claim that anything is your own."[13] In the second century A.D. Lucian, a severe critic of Christianity, wrote in *Peregrinus Proteus:*

> The activity of these people, in dealing with any matter that affects their community, is something extraordinary; they spare no trouble, no expense. . . . You see, these misguided creatures start with the general conviction that they are immortal for all time, which explains the contempt of death and voluntary self-devotion which are so common among them; and then it was impressed on them by their original lawgiver that they are all brothers, from the moment that they are converted, and deny the gods of Greece, and worship the crucified sage, and live after his laws. All this they take quite on trust, with the result that *they despise all worldly goods alike, regarding them merely as common property* (italics supplied).

Wouldn't it be nice if our worst critics said the same of our church!

Around the same time Justin Martyr wrote, "We who valued above all things the acquisition of wealth and possessions now bring what we have to a common stock, and communicate to everyone in need."[14] A generation later Tertullian declared, "The family possessions which generally destroy brotherhood among you, create fraternal bonds among us. One in mind and soul, we do not hesitate to share our earthly goods with one another. All things except our wives are common among us."[15] So even at the end of the second century Christians were still practicing communism to some degree.

But by the end of the fourth century Chrysostom was bemoaning the lapse of the church: "It is not for lack of miracles that the Church is staid, it is because we have forsaken the angelic life of Pentecost and fallen back on private property. If we lived as they did, with all things common, we should soon convert the whole world, without any need of miracles at all."[16]

Never again did the church as a whole enjoy such radical unity, although it cropped up in isolated areas at times. Today one of the salient aspects of primitive Christianity, communism, is missing from almost all current Protestant, Catholic, and even Eastern Orthodox practice.

* * *

Thus endeth the history lesson. Now for the practical application: How should we then live? This much seems clear: Is it too much to ask that Christians living today on the glory side of the cross might just barely manage to live up to Old Testament standards and contribute *at least* 10 percent of our income to God—in light of the fact that the earliest Christians gave 100 percent?

Tithing is not a goal. It is a minimum standard. Let me share with you the exciting story of one joy-filled Christian who discovered this.

Francis Chan is not a Seventh-day Adventist, but he is a believing child of God from whom we could learn a few things. He founded the Cornerstone Community Church in Simi Valley, California, in 1994 with only 30 people. By 2000 the church had grown to 1,600, later to 3,000.

I stumbled upon one of his sermon fragments that grabbed my attention. Pastor Chan shared a testimony of how God taught him that he could always trust the Lord to take care of him. He started out taking no income from the church, and then after the church grew he accepted a salary of $36,000 a year. Dozens of his members told him he needed to receive more. "You need to think of the cost of education for your kids."

"Well," he replied, "let's just see what God does first."

His refrigerator would break down, and a member would come by and say, "Hey, do you need a refrigerator? I bought two!" That sort of thing happened again and again.

His members continued to urge him to invest prudently for the future. But Chan saw the people living in crisis around the world, sometimes in need of just clean water, and felt that he should deny himself and take up his cross (just about the only saying of Jesus found in all four Gospels) and live as simply as possible today. Tomorrow, when his kids would be ready for college, God would provide scholarships if that's what He wanted them to do.

After one trip to Africa, he came back burdened with the need there, and sold his large house and moved into a much smaller place. The years that his family lived there would be the happiest in their lives.

Then Pastor Chan began to feel impressed that God wanted him to return

$50,000 back to Him. "Lord," he said, "I don't even make $50,000, but let's just see what happens." Unexpected money started to roll in, and he was able to give $50,000 that year!

The next year he sensed God challenging him to donate $100,000. Crazy things started taking place, and he presented God with $100,000.

Then—"God, are You kidding me?"—he came under the conviction that God wanted him to give to the Lord 1 million dollars! No way! But Chan's book *Crazy Love: Overwhelmed by a Relentless God* became a bestseller, and *sure enough* . . .

I think God was chuckling to Himself and saying, "Finally! Someone who gets it. Someone who really believes that I mean what I say, and that I keep My promises."

Eventually Pastor Chan gave away about 90 percent of his income, and accepted no income from his church. A few years ago Lisa Chan, Francis's wife, opened up their 1500-square-foot home—she claims it was plenty big for her four children—to another family of five in need. In fact, she gave them the master rooms so they could be more comfortable.

"Nothing in your life matters," Pastor Chan says, "except what you do for God. That's it. Every ounce of energy you spend on something else is a waste. Every dollar you spend on something else is a waste."

By the way, you might want to share Francis Chan's powerful presentation of the basic gospel for secular minds with an unbelieving friend. It has influenced hundreds of thousands in more than 30 countries. You'll find it at www.juststopandthink.com/.

---

1. See Friedrich Hauck, *Theological Dictionary of the New Testament,* eds. Gerhard Kittel and Gerhard Friedrich, trans. Geoffrey W. Bromiley (Grand Rapids: Eerdmans, 1965), vol. 3, pp. 789-809.

2. The Dead Sea scrolls use the term in 1QS 9:17-21; 1QS 10:21; 4Q400 frag. 1, col. 1:14-16; 4Q405 frag. 23, col. 1.

3. Josephus, *Wars of the Jews* 2.119-147.

4. Josephus, *Wars* 2.122; cf. *Antiquities of the Jews* 18.20ff. Philo says the same thing in *Quod Omnis Probus Liber* 85-87; *Apologia pro Judaeis* 11.4, 12.

5. 1QS 1:11-13; 4:24, 25, trans. G. Vermes.

6. Josephus, *Antiquities* 15.371.

7. Diogenes Laertius, *Lives of Eminent Philosophers* 1.8; 8. 8.

8. Malherbe, *The Cynic Epistles,* p. 233.

9. Aristotle, *Nicomachean Ethics* 8.9; *Politics* 2.6; 7.10.

10. Malherbe, p. 281.

11. Plato, *Laws* 5.739.

12. *Sibylline Oracles* 2.319-324.
13. Didache 4:8; Epistle of Barnabas 19:8.
14. Justin Martyr, *Apology* 1.14.2, 3.
15. Tertullian, *Apologeticus* 39.11.
16. John Chrysostom, *Homily* 25, on Acts.

# CHAPTER 10

# The Kingdom of Darkness

Since Luke is the main—in fact, the only—New Testament writer who clearly portrays the early Jesus movement as practicing the philosophy that began with Pythagoras of holding all things in common, and since this whole idea is bound to be highly controversial in some circles, it is important to explain modern Marxism. We must paint the stark contrast between Christian communism and modern atheistic Communism spelled with a capital *C*. It is the contrast between light and darkness.

The Orwellian horror known as Communism was born when the Adventist Church was born, and grew underground until it reared its ugly head in Russia in the Communist (Bolshevik) Revolution in the final year of World War I.

The eventual success of Communism was not because of Karl Marx, who was something of a ne'er-do-well, but because the god of this world was behind it. Marx was just his tool. Likewise, the success of the Seventh-day Adventist Church had very little to do with Ellen G. White—a devout but sickly woman with a third-grade education. No, God was behind it. Ellen White was simply His instrument. Both God and Satan use whomever they can to get the job done when the proper time comes.

It is a worthwhile study to show how the god of our world took something basically good and turned it into the antithesis of the kingdom of heaven. And therein lies a fascinating tale. You can't afford to ignore it, because it reveals a part of the great controversy that you probably never think about—a struggle swirling around you right out in the open, yet most Christians don't see it.

Let's start at the beginning.

Just before Karl Marx was born in 1818 his wealthy Jewish father, Heinrich Marx, became a Lutheran in order to continue practicing law following the Prussian edict denying Jews admittance to the bar. Young Karl saw that religion was merely a convenient profession that one could change on a whim for economic advantage. His father's hypocrisy, along with his college professors at Bonn and Berlin, made him an atheist.

At the university he fell in with the left-wing Hegelians who were consumed by a desire to liquidate Christianity. Marx wrote that he wanted to avenge himself "against the One who rules above." His stated model was the cry of Prometheus: "I hate all the gods!" His early writings mentioned the name "Oulanem," a ritualistic name for Satan. A friend wrote in 1841 that "Marx calls the Christian religion one of the most immoral of religions." He and Bruno Bauer decided to publish a *Journal of Atheism* but could find no financial sponsors.

One of his letters to the woman he hoped to wed gives us some idea of the man. "Jenny, if we can but weld our souls together, then with contempt shall I fling my glove in the world's face, then shall I stride through the wreckage a creator." They were married in June 1843.

Though he wanted to run the world, Marx could not run his own family. Incapable of holding down a job, he was forever in debt, in spite of the financial support of his closest friend Friedrich Engels. His bankruptcies and revolutionary activities resulted in his expulsion from one country after another. Marx fled from Germany to France to Belgium and finally to a London slum, where he spent his time in the British Museum library as his wife and children starved. His daughter Franziska and his son Edgar died. Another baby died at birth. Later on his daughter Eleanor ran away with a young man and then committed suicide. Another daughter, Laura, married a doctor then committed suicide. Then his wife, Jenny, and his favorite daughter, Jenny, died. Two months later Marx was dead. But not before he had changed the world.

Before Marx no communism was atheistic; it was religious in principle. During the 1840s the largest organization with communist ideals in Europe was the League of the Just, whose motto was "All Men Are Brothers" and whose aim was to establish a new society "based on the ideals of love of one's neighbor, equality and justice." Marx and Engels, both of whom became 32nd degree Masons, joined the League in 1847. Under their influence the organization turned secular and activist, and changed its name to the Communist League. At the invitation of the League, the pair produced in 1848 a political tract now known as the *Communist Manifesto,* which during the next century would become enormously influential.

Among other things, the *Manifesto* advocated the abolition of private property; elimination of the family; a heavy progressive or graduated income tax; abolition of all rights of inheritance; centralization of credit in the hands of the state with a national bank; centralization and state control of all communication and transportation; the elimination of child factory labor and free education for all children in public schools; and the abolition of all religion. You might want to think about how far down this road your country has already come. It might give you nightmares.

Marxist Communism went on to inflict untold suffering on the world. Some estimate that Joseph Stalin and Mao Tse-tung alone were responsible for the deaths of more than 100 million people between them. For a litany of the ghastly horrors of the last century, you may read *The Black Book of Communism,* or Paul Hollander's *From the Gulag to the Killing Fields,* but I wouldn't advise it. You should, however, read W. Cleon Skousen, *The Naked Communist,* or Peter Hitchens, *The Rage Against God: How Atheism Led me to Faith.*

Atheistic, coercive, and violent, Marxist Communism is an overturning of the moral order. Alexander Solzhenitsyn observed, "Communism has never concealed the fact that it rejects all absolute concepts of morality. It scoffs at any consideration of 'good' and 'evil' as indisputable categories. Communism considers morality to be relative, to be a class matter. Depending upon circumstances and the political situation, any act, including murder, even the killing of hundreds of thousands, could be good or could be bad. It all depends upon class ideology."

Marxist Communism also puts forward a new moral value—equality, something never considered a virtue either in traditional societies or in Scripture, not even within the church.[1] Unity, yes, but not equality. Notice how God dealt with the demand for equality on the part of Korah, Dathan, and Abiram (Num. 16:3) by opening up a special pit just for them (verses 32-35).

One of the mottoes of the French Revolution had been "*Liberte* [freedom], *Egalite* [equality], *Fraternite* [brotherhood]." How well did that work out? Under the rubric of "reason" Maximilien Robespierre and the Jacobins beheaded 40,000 French citizens during 1793-1794.

Vladimir Lenin took his cue from Marx, advocating such violence: "It will be necessary to repeat the year 1793. After achieving power we'll be considered monsters, but we couldn't care less." He and his cohorts described themselves as "glorious Jacobins." That's "reason" and "equality" without God.

So consistently do evil social movements appeal to this alleged virtue that we begin to suspect that the demand for equality is one of the original heresies of Lucifer before he was expelled from heaven. If so, it worked well. Perhaps it was by demanding equality for all that Satan won the allegiance of one-third of the angels (Rev. 12:4). They bought the lie from the father of lies, having never heard a lie before, and because they were not satisfied with the place God assigned them, they lost even what they had.

Millions still fall for the lie today. Equality is a very seductive idea, because it sounds so noble. Making equality a right spreads hatred by making the have-nots envious of the haves. This hatred between social classes is an attack on the basic American principle of *e pluribus unum* ("many become one"), a principle also essential to Christianity (see John 17:20-23; Eph. 2:11, 12; Gal. 3:28).

At the same time Communism nullifies the tenth commandment, recasting envy as a virtue instead of a sin. Perhaps the reason Christianity has traditionally considered envy as one of the seven deadly sins is because of the deadly effect it has on any society. When various races or classes start envying one another, both civility and prosperity disappear. And since atheism inevitably tends toward survival of the fittest, Communism becomes a way for the politically powerful to steal not only from the "robber barons" but also from those who have acquired wealth through virtue and hard work and who provide jobs for others. As a result, it deprives thousands of workers of their livelihood and their self-respect, making them wards of the state, which increases the dictatorial power of the state and at the same time impoverishes it.

Winston Churchill put it this way: "The inherent vice of capitalism is the unequal sharing of blessings; the inherent virtue of socialism is the equal sharing of miseries."

Suppose you don't have enough pie to go around. Capitalism asks, How can I make more pie? Marxism asks, How can I divide the pie equally? That requires redistribution of wealth, forcing the producers to pay for the non-producers. By penalizing success, you get less of it. By subsidizing failure, you create more of it. That leads to poverty by robbing human beings of the motivation to better themselves. To see why, let's try a simple mental experiment.

Ask a group of students in any classroom if they would be willing, on a trial basis, to have all grades averaged for one semester, with everyone receiving the average grade of the class. Usually more than half will agree. After all, why should some be rewarded above others for their natural endowments? Why not take from the haves and give to the have-nots? No student needs to feel inferior anymore. We're all equal now.

With no incentives for trying hard, and no penalties for slacking off, human nature takes over. The class average declines through time, until the whole class is . . . well, underperforming. We have produced an entire population of demotivated slackers by encouraging envy instead of prohibiting it.

That is why Communist nations become economic basket cases until they adopt elements of capitalism. Capitalism motivates by allowing each individual to get as far as possible, and the successful are expected to help those who have fallen behind. The result of setting people free to pursue their goals and be all that they can be leads to a greater measure of wealth for all. In capitalist countries even poor individuals are comparatively rich. The very poorest Americans are wealthier than 60 percent of the world's population, according to a recent World Bank study.[2]

Jesus understood this principle. His parable of the minas in Luke 19:11-27 is based on capitalistic presuppositions. It involves buying, selling, and trading at a profit. In the parable the best producers receive the greatest rewards, and the one who refuses to work loses even what he has. His little gets confiscated and goes to the best producer. In the parable the king actually takes from the poor and gives to the rich! Something to think about.

But under the leadership of the prince of darkness, Communism's goal is to turn societies that have a major Christian presence, such as America or Brazil or South Korea, into atheistic, despairing, alcoholic, corrupt states. This conspiracy is not on a human level but on a supernatural one. We wrestle not against flesh and blood.

If you want to study the nefarious process by which a nation is converted to Communism, study the works of two men: Ion Mihai Pacepa, the highest-ranking Soviet bloc intelligence official ever to defect to the West (in 1978), who wrote *Disinformation* (2013); and Yuri Bezmenov, a KGB propagandist who defected to the West in 1970, whose lectures are available on YouTube.

According to these men, the main interest of the Soviet KGB was not espionage but propaganda. Eighty-five percent of their efforts were devoted to ideological subversion. It was not blowing up bridges, but blowing up a traditional culture.

The first and longest stage, demoralization, now completed in the United States, is followed by destabilization, then crisis, then renormalization under Communism. As you learn the techniques used to achieve these steps you will see them all around you. That is one benefit of being educated in a Seventh-day Adventist educational institution. Most institutions of higher education in America today teach Marxism.

\* \* \*

America won a major battle against this ideology with the fall of the Soviet Union in 1991. How did that happen? Well, the cause wasn't just American military expenditures that the Soviet Union could not match, or Ronald

Reagan's call to tear down the wall. A major factor in this victory was the invisible hand of God, invoked by a huge prayer campaign in Europe. Here is the largely forgotten story of how prayer felled Communism in Europe.

November 9, 1989, will be remembered as the day the Berlin Wall came down. But it was actually a prayer meeting held exactly one month earlier that made its collapse inevitable. You will find the story in an article authored by Peter Crutchley, available online.[3]

"Ignoring death threats and huge banks of armed police, thousands gathered at St. Nicholas Church in the East German city of Leipzig on October 9 to pray for peace. The congregation then joined an estimated crowd of 70,000 on a protest march against the country's Communist regime."

Although "the largest impromptu demonstration ever witnessed in East Germany, [it] was no spontaneous flash mob." Rather, "it was the culmination of years of weekly prayer meetings organized by Christian Führer, the pastor of St. Nicholas."

"Disillusioned with the Berlin Wall, the physical fault line of the ongoing Cold War and the repressive East German regime, Pastor Führer began organizing Prayers for Peace every Monday evening, beginning in 1982."

Sometimes "fewer than a dozen people attended the prayer meetings. The East German government strongly discouraged its citizens from becoming involved in religious activities," but they ignored these meetings at first as insignificant. Monday after Monday they plodded on. Then they began to swell. As the scale of the gatherings grew, the government began to pressure the pastor to stop the meetings, but he remained resolute.

"Momentum began to build in earnest" after May 1989, when "the authorities barricaded the streets leading to the church," hoping to discourage people from attending, "but it had the opposite effect. . . . By this time the prayer meetings had led to a series of peaceful political protests in Leipzig and other cities [that] became known as the Monday Demonstrations."

"Things came to a head on October 7, 1989, the fortieth anniversary of the German Democratic Republic." Police made "hundreds of arrests . . . among the crowds in front of the Nikolai Church." Erich Honecker, the brutal Communist leader of East Germany, ordered the church closed.

"An article appeared in a local newspaper announcing" that the government would put down the counterrevolution on Monday, October 9, "with whatever means necessary." Tens of thousands of troops appeared in the square, determined to create another Tiananmen Square massacre if necessary. They prepared the hospitals for the bloodbath by sending them extra supplies and set aside large stadiums for those arrested. The Christians understood the danger, so couples left one member at home with their children so that someone would survive and take care of them afterward.

"On October 9, 1989, as Leipzigers returned home from work, they saw the city fill with soldiers and police, increasing the sense of foreboding" and fear. One woman later related how she lost custody of her children for a while. The authorities even threatened to put her youngest daughter into a children's home. The official documents charged that she was unfit as a mother because she participated in extremist groups.

"Up to 8,000 crowded into St. Nicholas Church, including members of the feared Stasi (secret police) who had been sent to occupy it. Other Leipzig churches opened to accommodate additional protesters. About 70,000 people had now gathered in the city.

"After an hour-long service at St. Nicholas, Pastor Führer led worshipers outside." Demonstrators clutching lit candles filled the nearby Augustusplatz. "Slowly the crowd began walking around the city, past the Stasi headquarters, chanting 'We are the people' and 'No violence,' accompanied by thousands of helmeted riot police ready to intervene."

"Massacre was just minutes away." Then at the last moment a deal was struck, and the police stood aside and let the protesters march by. "The dam had burst."

Pastor Führer said: "They didn't attack. They had nothing to attack for. East German officials would later say they were ready for anything, except for candles and prayer."

The media widely broadcast footage of the march, "which inspired Monday Demonstrations throughout East Germany [during] the following weeks."

"About 120,000 people took to the streets the following Monday. Erich Honecker resigned two days later. . . . Exactly a month after the events of October 9 the Berlin Wall came down amid scenes of jubilation witnessed around the world."

"The people who came to demonstrate on October 9," Pastor Führer said, "came from all over East Germany. Without Leipzig, the Berlin Wall would not have fallen, let alone the reunification of Germany. What moved me the most was that people who had grown up in two atheist dictatorships—first the Nazis then the Communist regimes—were able to distill the message of Jesus into two words: no violence. Without the church it would have been like all other revolutions before—bloody and unsuccessful."

That is how Christians tear down strongholds. Love, truth, and prayer are the most powerful weapons on earth.

After the fall of the Berlin Wall, St. Nicholas went back to being a normal parish church. Pastor Führer pastored the church until his retirement in 2009. The weekly prayers for peace continue.

Another East German pastor, Uwe Holmer, and his wife led a Christian community for mentally disabled indiviuals, seniors, and those with epilepsy near East Berlin. Because of their pastoral activities, the Holmers had suffered terribly during the long reign of Dictator Honecker. In late 1989 Honecker left office as perhaps one of the most hated men alive: no one would take the ailing despot in, not even his own daughter.

Finally, the Holmers gave shelter to Honecker and his wife, deposed Education minister Margot Honecker. Pastor Holmer's explanation for his seemingly irrational behavior in taking in the very couple who had caused him and eight of his ten children untold suffering was simple enough: "The Lord has charged us to follow Him and to take in all those who are troubled or burdened . . . to follow His commandment to love our enemies; and to live by the prayer He taught us in these words: 'forgive us our trespasses as we forgive those who trespass against us.' . . . We want to live by Christ's example."

Most people think that in 1989 with the fall of the Berlin Wall and then the collapse of the Soviet Union in 1991, America won the war against Communism. But it didn't. It only won a battle. Ideologies are not so easily stamped out. Marxism and Leninism did not dry up and blow away overnight. Instead, they went underground. Gay marriage is only the latest victory, a Communist goal here for some time. It will continue to attack until replaced by a darker power that stands not against but within the temple of God (2 Thess. 2:4).

* * *

Wouldn't it be nice if we could conduct a massive experiment with the philosophies of Communism and capitalism? Starting with the same culture and tradition, let half of the country try Communism, and the other half capitalism, and see which worked best?

Well, it's been done! Korea had a monolithic culture before the Korean War. Afterward the nation was poverty-stricken, with only one paved road in what is now South Korea. The per capita income was only $80 a year. Farmers would starve before the next crop came in. Then North Korea fell under Communism, where government-enforced "equality" makes everyone equally miserable to this day, and Christianity endures severe persecution.

But by its intervention in the Korean War, America saved South Korea from the same fate, and both Christianity and capitalism flourished. Today South Korea is one of the world's richest nations. You can actually see the difference in nighttime satellite photographs: North Korea is a sea of darkness, while South Korea is ablaze with light. Korea's best smartphone (Samsung Galaxy) vies for first place with America's best (Apple iPhone).

The nation's rising prosperity parallels the explosive growth of Christianity. In the year 1900 only a handful of Koreans were Christians. By 1945 it had grown to only about 2 percent of the populace. Today, even though non-Christians still outnumber Christians, Seoul has nine of the 11 largest Christian megachurches in the world, and Korea is awash with prayer, sending out more missionaries than any country except America and possibly Brazil. In Seoul one can find large congregations meeting at five in the morning for prayer, with no empty seats in their 5,000-seat sanctuaries.

Korea's prosperity stems from many reasons, including strong national leadership, but one contributing factor is religious faith. Devotion to God usually leads a nation, in the long run, to riches. That's not health-and-wealth theology; it's the theology of John Wesley (1703-1791), who said: "I do not see how it is possible, in the nature of things, for any revival of true religion to continue long. For religion must necessarily produce both industry and frugality, and these cannot but produce riches. But as riches increase, so will pride, anger, and love of the world in all its branches." Wesley was skeptical that spirituality and prosperity could long coexist. And it is true that the growth of the Korean church has gradually slowed in the past few years.

The Adventist Church has prospered there too. Today Sahmyook University in Seoul is the largest Seventh-day Adventist university on earth, with six colleges, 216 full-time faculty, 5,566 undergraduate students, and 189 graduate students. Each January more than 10,000 students apply, of which only about 12 percent get accepted as new students. Only one in six of them are Adventists.

But it had small beginnings. It was founded in 1906 as a tiny Seventh-day Adventist school, Euimyung College, in what would become today's North Korea. It was the first higher education facility started in Korea. Back in the days before World War I, when Euimyung College was struggling, Japan invaded Korea and colonized it. During those early years of the twentieth century it wasn't Communism but Shintoism that led to the brutal treatment of the few Christians in Korea. The Japanese boarded up the evangelical churches, ejected foreign missionaries, and jailed key Christian leaders. Adventist missionaries stopped managing their whole school system, because the

Japanese rulers enforced Shinto worship, and Euimyung College eventually had to close for a time.

The ruthless persecution intensified around 1919. Tim Kimmel, in his book *Little House on the Freeway,* tells the riveting story of a little white wooden frame church in Korea that endured a holocaust of hate. "One pastor persistently entreated his local Japanese police chief for permission to meet for services. His nagging was finally accommodated, and the police chief offered to unlock his church—for one last meeting." The word soon spread, and "committed Christians starving for an opportunity of unhindered worship quickly made plans. Long before dawn on that promised Sunday, Korean families [from] throughout the region made their way" past the cold eyes of the Japanese overlords to the church.

"The Korean church has always had a reputation as a singing church. As they closed the doors behind them, they shut out their anxieties, and the little wooden frame sanctuary rang with praise and thanksgiving. For a handful of peasants listening nearby, the final two songs [this congregation sang] seemed . . . suspended in time.

"It was during a stanza of 'Nearer, My God, to Thee' that the Japanese police chief waiting outside gave the orders." The people toward the back of the church heard the doors being barricaded and began to smell the odor of kerosene mingled with smoke. "The dried wooden skin of the small church quickly ignited. Fumes filled the structure as tongues of flame began to lick the baseboard of the interior walls."

Immediately people rushed for the windows. But the moment of hope turned to despair "as the men climbing out the windows came crashing back in—their bodies ripped in a hail of bullets."

"The good pastor knew it was the end." With a calm confidence, "he led his congregation in a hymn whose words served as a fitting farewell to earth and a loving salutation to heaven. The first few words were all the prompting the terrified worshipers needed. With smoke burning their eyes, they joined as one to sing of their hope and leave their legacy. There song became a serenade to the horrified and helpless witnesses outside."

"Alas! and did my Savior bleed?
And did my Sovereign die?
Would He devote that sacred head for such a worm as I?"

Just before the roof collapsed they sang the last verse, their final testament of faith:

"But drops of grief can ne'er repay the debt of love I owe:
Here, Lord, I give myself away
'Tis all that I can do!
At the cross, at the cross where I first saw the light,
And the burden of my heart rolled away—
It was there by faith I received my sight,
And now I am happy all the day."

Then the dying strains of music and wails of children vanished in a roar of flames.

"Clearing the incinerated remains was the easy part. Erasing the hate would take decades." For many of the relatives of the victims nothing could ever atone for the carnage. "Evil had stooped to a new low," and their loathing of the Japanese now knew no limits. Long after the fire died to ashes, the flames of hatred burned within many Korean hearts.

When the Japanese withdrew their forces at the end of the war, the Koreans built a memorial to the slain Christians on the very spot the church once stood. But that monument also served as a "mute reminder of their pain," and a perpetual fountain of their soul-shackling bitterness now passed on to a new generation.

In 1971 "a group of Japanese pastors traveling through Korea" chanced upon that memorial. "When they read the details of the tragedy and the names of the spiritual brothers and sisters who had perished, they were overcome with shame. Their country had sinned, and even though none of them were personally involved, . . . they still felt a national guilt that could not be excused."

They returned to Japan committed to right a wrong. There came "an immediate outpouring of love from their fellow believers," who raised 10 million yen, enough to build a beautiful white church building on the site of the tragedy.

A delegation of Japanese Christians attended the dedication service for the new building. During the service the Korean representatives acknowledged the Japanese generosity and appreciated their attempts at making peace, yet the painful memories made reconciliation impossible. The wounds still festered. Hatreds nourished for decades could not easily and quickly surrender. "Christian brothers or not, [the Japanese visitors] were descendants of a ruthless enemy."

Dignitaries made speeches, recalled the details of the tragedy, and honored the names of the dead. It came time to bring the service to a close. Someone in charge of the agenda thought it would be appropriate to conclude with the same two songs sung the day the church burned.

The song leader began the words to "Nearer, My God, to Thee." As the voices mingled in familiar melody, and the "memories of the past mixed with the truth of the [lyrics], resistance started to melt." The inspiration that gave hope to a doomed congregation in a past generation now offered hope once more.

"The song leader closed the service with the hymn 'At the Cross.' The normally stoic Japanese could not contain themselves. The tears that [began] to fill their eyes during the song suddenly gushed from deep inside. They turned to their Korean [brothers and sisters] and begged them for forgiveness." The Koreans hesitated, "but the love of the Japanese believers . . . tore at the Koreans' emotions."

"At the cross, at the cross where I first saw the light,
And the burden of my heart rolled away . . ."

One Korean turned toward a Japanese brother. Then another. Suddenly the floodgates burst, and a wave of emotion swept over the crowd. "The Koreans met their new Japanese friends in the middle. They clung to each other and wept. Japanese tears of repentance and Korean tears of forgiveness" bathed the wounds of bitterness and hatred, leaving only reconciliation and love.[4]

What philosophy, what sort of power was it that washed away such hatred? It was not psychiatry or psychology that did it. No, it was an old rugged cross. And why is the cross such an effective antidote to darkness and hatred? Because it bears the image of a Man whose hands were stretched out wide from east to west, as if grasping and embracing those two polar opposites and drawing them together. When Jesus said, "Father, forgive them," He reached beyond that wooden bar down through time and across cultures and grasped alienated hearts everywhere and made them whole, made them one. Those who nailed His holy hands to that rough timber believed they were confining Him, restricting Him, immobilizing Him, but instead they were releasing Him, extending Him, magnifying Him until He filled all time and eternity. When He died, Jesus grabbed us by the heart, and I pray that He will never let go.

\* \* \*

"The light shines in the darkness, and the darkness has not overcome it" (John 1:5, NIV). In Germany, in Korea, the light vanquished the darkness. And now, wonder of wonders, it is beginning to happen in China.

In 1949 Communism took over China and set out to eradicate faith. By 1958 Mao's wife, Jiang Qing, told foreign visitors, "Christianity in China . . . is dead and buried." During the 1970s a visiting Christian delegation from the United States reported, "There is not a single Christian left in China."[5] The few remaining were all in hiding.

But then came the resurrection of faith. Today, while the Chinese Communist Party has 82 million members, the Christian church is estimated at more than 100 million. Lower estimates are unreliable because most Chinese Christians stay hidden, as they still face persecution.

Growth since the beginning of the twenty-first century has been amazingly rapid. Today nearly a million new Christians get baptized in China *every month.* And they are sending missionaries into North Korea and all across the globe.

In a few years China will have more Christians any other nation on earth. Fenggang Yang, a professor of sociology at Purdue University and author of *Religion in China: Survival and Revival Under Communist Rule,* estimates that by 2025 the number of Protestants alone will be 160 million, exceeding the United States total.

China's revived Christianity has been purified through persecution. It is aglow. And it is unstoppable. Communism is in a death struggle with Christianity, tearing down some of the largest Christian churches in mid-2014. It must sense that its days are numbered.

Now I am no prophet, but I have a hunch. If America should become a persecuting power, and "repudiate every principle of its Constitution as a Protestant and republican government,"[6] I suspect that God may be preparing China to be the next great Christian superpower. China has the world's second largest economy. It poured more concrete in a recent three-year period than America did in the entire twentieth century, according to historian Vaclav Smil. And China refuses to allow Google to purvey pornography on its servers, so in common moral sense it is already ahead of us in some ways. It is possible that God has planned for all those sparkling new empty cities in China to become cities of refuge for persecuted Christians from around the world. If you are young and our Lord doesn't return soon, perhaps you should consider learning Mandarin.

Christ is the victor, and we triumph with Him if we stay by His side, even sharing His suffering. We can resist the mighty forces of evil through the power of PLT: prayer, love, and truth. Those weapons are mightier by far than the powers of darkness. "The weapons we fight with . . . have divine power to demolish strongholds" (2 Cor. 10:4, NIV).

Jesus launched a counterrevolution to the ideology of evil. Our task is to do the same for the kingdom of light that Communism does for the kingdom of darkness. We find the recipe for this given in Jesus' shortest parable, found in Matthew 13:33: "The kingdom of heaven is like yeast that a woman took and mixed into about sixty pounds of flour until it worked all through the dough" (NIV). The gospel of Jesus Christ and Communism are both like leaven. They gradually permeate a culture.

So where do you come in?

You are a secret agent for the kingdom. Your task, if you should accept it, is to spread the light, without guile, without force, with the same zeal that the evil powers of our world spread hate and darkness. You should pray for souls. Selflessly love them into fellowship. And you should give them God's truth, disseminating it throughout the culture. The proper order is important; they must be prayed for and loved before they are willing to hear the truth.

My friend, someplace near you darkness is soon to fall, but Jesus is victor! For millions the darkness is already here. But if you are reading this book, you possess the most powerful weapons ever given to mortal human beings in the fight against evil: prayer, love, and truth. Use them while you have the light. You are on the winning side.

All the darkness cannot extinguish one candle. You are that candle.

Just glow!

---

1. "Obey your leaders and submit to them" (Heb. 13:17, ESV); "Wives, submit to your husbands" (Col. 3:18, ESV); "You are younger, be subject to your elders" (1 Pet. 5:5, ESV).

2. See Dylan Matthews, "This Chart Might Make You Feel Better About American Inequality," *Washington Post*, Aug. 15, 2013.

3. Peter Crutchley, "Did a Prayer Meeting Really Bring Down the Berlin Wall?" www.bbc.co.uk/religion/0/24661333.

4. Tim Kimmel, *Little House on the Freeway* (Colorado Springs, Colo.: Multnomah Books, 2008), pp. 51-55.

5. Brother Yun and Paul Hattaway, *The Heavenly Man* (Oxford, England: Monarch Books /Lion Hudson, 2002), p. 7.

6. Ellen G. White, *Testimonies for the Church* (Mountain View, Calif.: Pacific Press Pub. Assn., 1948), vol. 5, p. 451.

# CHAPTER 11

# The Kingdom of Light

In the previous chapter we explained the difference between the kingdom of darkness and the kingdom of light as they manifest themselves today in our world. This chapter is more theoretical. We want to go back and see if we can understand exactly what Jesus had in mind when He preached the kingdom. And what a first-century Jew who heard Him would think He was talking about. You might be surprised at the answer.

In the Synoptic Gospels (Matthew, Mark, and Luke) Jesus not only calls Himself the Son of man, but He speaks of the *coming* of the Son of man (Matt. 10:23; 16:27, 28; 24:27, 30, 37, 39, 44; 25:31; 26:64; Mark 8:38; 9:1; 13:26; 14:62; Luke 9:26; 12:40; 17:24; 18:8; 21:27).

He also describes the Son of man as arriving *in the clouds* (Mark 13:26; 14:62; Matt. 26:64; 24:30; Luke 21:27).

Furthermore, He has much to say about the *kingdom* of the Son of man (Matt. 13:41; 16:28; 25:31-34; Mark 8:38-9:1; Luke 9:26, 27; 17:20-30).

All of these passages are clear allusions to Daniel 7:13, 14: "In my vision at night I looked, and there before me was one like a *son of man, coming with the clouds of heaven.* He approached the Ancient of Days and was led into his presence. He was given authority, glory and sovereign power; all nations and peoples of every language worshiped him. His dominion is an everlasting dominion that will not pass away, and *his kingdom* is one that will never be destroyed" (NIV).

*Daniel 7:13, 14 is the single most important passage in all of pre-Christian literature for understanding Christian origins.* Jesus alluded to it more than any other passage. It provided Him with His title and told of His coming and His kingdom. One might even suggest that Christianity began when the young Jesus first began to contemplate Daniel 7:13, 14.

The Old Testament mentions the concept of a kingdom that belongs to God in several places, but only in passing. However, Daniel 2 and 7 develop the concept at length.

Notice that Daniel 2 explains Jesus' terminology in Matthew 21:43, 44: "Therefore I tell you that the kingdom of God will be taken away from you and *given to a people* who will produce its fruit. Anyone who falls on this stone will be *broken to pieces;* anyone on whom it falls will be *crushed"* (NIV; cf. Luke 20:16-18). Lay this alongside Daniel 2:44, 45: "In the time of those kings, the God of heaven will set up a kingdom that will never be destroyed, nor will it be *left to another people.* It will *crush* all those kingdoms and bring them to an end, but it will itself endure forever. This is the meaning of the vision of the rock cut out of a mountain, but not by human hands—a rock that *broke* the iron, the bronze, the clay, the silver and the gold *to pieces"* (NIV).

The "broken/crushed" terminology in Matthew 21 is the conclusion to Jesus' parable of the vineyard (Mark 12:1-11; Matt. 21:33-44). The parable involves a play on words between the son (Hebrew *ben*) of the owner of the vineyard and the stone (Hebrew and Aramaic *eben*) of Daniel 2, which had acquired Messianic overtones by New Testament times in light of Psalm 118:22, 23; Isaiah 8:14; 28:16; and Zechariah 4:7-10. Jesus is identifying Himself with the stone of Daniel 2. The rabbis also equated the stone of Daniel 2 with "King Messiah."[1]

What is the point of all these references? Just this: *When Jesus started preaching about the kingdom He had no need to explain it, because it was already a predefined concept.* The kingdom of God was the fifth kingdom of Daniel 7. When at the outset of His ministry He proclaimed, "The time has come. . . . The kingdom of God has come near" (Mark 1:15, NIV), His audience would surely have understood the allusion to Daniel 7:22: "The time came for the saints to possess the kingdom" (NKJV).

There seems to be no end to the flood of scholarly treatises addressing the apparently complicated question of what Jesus meant by the kingdom. But they routinely overlook the simplest answer. *The kingdom originally proclaimed by John the Baptist and Jesus was the kingdom of God in Daniel 2 and 7,* shaped by the eschatology of Isaiah. Jesus did not invent the idea, He merely fleshed out the concept He found in Scripture. It was Daniel's apocalyptic kingdom that Jesus preached as being at hand.

Many Jews already knew that, in general, it was time for the kingdom—the fifth empire of Daniel 7—to commence and bring an end to the reign of the fourth empire. The fourth empire, they knew, was Rome.[2] Rome had been around for centuries, so it was high time for the kingdom of God to come.

Neither Jesus nor the apostles ever dispute this timetable. They never urged repentance because "life is short." They seem to have believed that the end of time was nearer than the end of life: "The night is nearly over; the day is almost here" (Rom. 13:12, NIV); "The God of peace will soon crush Satan under your feet" (Rom. 16:20, NIV); "The time is short. . . . This world in its present form is passing away" (1 Cor. 7:29-31, NIV); "These things . . . were written down as warnings for us, on whom the culmination ["end"; cf. Heb. 9:26] of the ages has come" (1 Cor. 10:11, NIV); "The Lord is near" (Phil. 4:5, NIV); "In just a little while, he who is coming will come and will not delay" (Heb. 10:37, NIV); "The Lord's coming is near. . . . The Judge is standing at the door" (James 5:8, 9, NIV); "They will give an account to Him who is ready to judge the living and the dead. . . . The end of all things is at hand. . . . The time has come for judgment to begin at the house of God" (1 Pet. 4:5-17, NKJV); "This is the last hour" (1 John 2:18, NIV); "The hour of his judgment has come" (Rev. 14:7, NIV).

The entire Gospel tradition leans heavily upon Daniel 7:13, 14. When Jesus promised His interrogators that they would see the Son of man coming with the clouds of heaven (Mark 14:62; Matt. 26:64), His listeners would no doubt have understood Him to refer to the great event described in Daniel 7:13. One passage intelligible only in light of Daniel 7:13, 14 is John 5:27: "And he [God] has given him authority to judge because he is the Son of Man" (NIV).

Early Christianity viewed the prophesied kingdom as the fifth kingdom of Daniel 7, which explains why the ultimate goal of Jesus, according to Paul, was to "destroy all dominion, authority and power" (1 Cor. 15:24, NIV; cf. Eph. 1:10). To Him every knee would bow (Rom. 14:11; Phil. 2:10). Jesus Christ is "the ruler of the kings of the earth" (Rev. 1:5, NIV). He would "rule them with an iron scepter" (Rev. 2:27, NIV; 12:7). Since that would require force, it is why Jesus would return "with power" or "in force" (Mark 9:1; Matt. 24:30; 2 Pet. 1:16; cf. 1 Enoch 1:4).

Usually we don't think of the kingdom in terms of force. Wait a minute. Yes, we do. All Christians are familiar with Revelation 19's portrait of Jesus returning with a sword in His mouth to tread down the nations.

But today is still the day of grace, and so we emphasize the gentle gospel that wins men and women to the kingdom. God will take care of the hard stuff. Our task is that of loving them to Him. He postpones the hard stuff so that He can save a few more.

Here is a burning question: Has the kingdom of heaven ever actually come? Scholars have long debated the question. German scholars, led by J. Weiss and A. Schweitzer around the turn of the twentieth century, claimed the kingdom never came. A line of British scholars, starting in the 1930s with C. H. Dodd, his student G. B. Caird, and Caird's student, N. T. Wright, say that it has indeed arrived, and we need expect no future cataclysm. Jesus will never literally return in the clouds. He only comes to each of us when we accept Him.

But the modern consensus, first expressed by W. G. Kummel in the 1940s, is both yes and no. Some of the prophecies associated with the kingdom came to pass while others did not. Although Jesus has not yet arrived in the clouds, the New Testament seems to assume implicitly that the coronation of Daniel 7:13, 14 is a past event that took place after the Resurrection (see Matt. 28:18; John 17:2; Acts 5:31; 7:56; Eph. 1:20-22; 1 Pet. 3:22; cf. Dan. 7:27, LXX; Rev. 5:6-10). And some passages regard the kingdom as already begun (Rom. 14:17; 1 Cor. 4:20; Col. 1:13; Rev. 1:6, 9; 5:10; 12:10). In fact, Paul can even speak of the resurrection of the believer as if it were history (e.g., Eph. 2:6).

However, this is prolepsis: "God . . . calls those things which do not exist as though they did" (Rom. 4:17, NKJV). He brings the future into the present. Well-known final events are said to be already present, at least in a spiritual sense. Jesus said Elijah has already come. John announced that the antichrist was already present and that we even now have "eternal life." Paul declared that we are already raised up with Christ.

The fact remains, however, that the apostolic witnesses usually place the kingdom in the future (Acts 1:6; 14:22; 1 Cor. 6:9; 15:20, 28, 50; Gal. 5:21; Eph. 5:5; 2 Thess. 1:5; 2 Tim. 4:1, 18; Heb. 12:28; 2 Pet. 1:11; Rev. 11:15).

And two additional themes, often forgotten in discussions on this topic, should settle the matter. Paul clearly states that we are still living in the old age (Rom. 12:2; 1 Cor. 1:20; 2:6, 8; 3:18; Gal. 1:4). And the ruler of the world is still Satan (John 12:31; 14:30; 16:11; 2 Cor. 4:4; Eph. 2:2; 6:12; 1 John 5:19). Clearly, then, the kingdom has not yet come.

E. P. Sanders states, "If . . . we have to choose between 'present' and 'future' as emphases in Jesus' message, we must, on the basis of present evidence, put the emphasis on the kingdom as immediately future."[3]

That is why the Seventh-day Adventist Church places so much focus on the Second Coming. Until then, the kingdom is present only as a shadow of things to come.

An instructional passage here is Hebrews 8:6-13. While Jesus is Mediator of the new covenant (verse 6), the old, obsolete covenant is still operative—it has not yet disappeared (verse 13). Clearly the time has not yet arrived when no one needs to teach their neighbor to know the Lord (verse 11). The ultimate fulfillment of the promise "I will be their God, and they will be my people" (verse 10, NIV) is still future (Rev. 21:3, 7). According to Paul, the adoption as sons for which we are predestined (Eph. 1:5) is in some ways something that we still await (Rom. 8:23). However, the "I will forgive their sins" aspect is a present reality (Heb. 10:14-18).

Our answer to the question of the kingdom determines our response to the issue of the law. If "all has been accomplished" and the kingdom is fully here, and the law is written on every heart (Heb. 8:10; 10:16), then the external law is obsolete. But if not, then the law has an ongoing function, as implied in Romans 2:13-15, 26, 27; 3:31; 8:4; 13:8-10; 1 Corinthians 7:19; 9:21; Galatians 3:24; 5:14; 6:2; 1 Timothy 1:8-10; James 1:25; 2:8-12; 4:11; 1 John 5:2, 3; and Revelation 12:17; 14:12. The law continues to function as a moral standard, but not as a means of salvation. This has been the emerging consensus among New Testament scholars ever since 1979, when C. E. B. Cranfield published *A Critical and Exegetical Commentary on the Epistle to the Romans,* which concludes, "For Paul, the law is not abrogated by Christ."[4]

In the Synoptic Gospels the kingdom comes when the Son of man returns. Thus Mark 13:29 and Matthew 24:33 say that "when you see all these things happening" then "it" (the *parousia*) is near, while the parallel in Luke 21:31 says the "kingdom" is near. Likewise, Mark 9:1 and Luke 9:27 state that "some who are standing here will not taste death before they see the kingdom of God" (NIV), whereas the previous verses (Mark 8:38; Luke 9:26), as well as the parallel in Matthew 16:28, speak of the coming of the Son of man. That the kingdom follows the *parousia* also appears in Matthew 7:21-23; 8:11; 25:34; 26:29; Mark 14:25; and Luke 22:15-18, 29, 30. Acts 14:22 suggests that the kingdom lies on the other side of the tribulation.

In short, those who say that the kingdom has never come have the better part of the argument. Clearly the time has not yet happened when wolf and lion lie down with lamb and calf, and a child leads them (Isa. 11:6). Jerusalem is not a place of peace, and the knowledge of the Lord does not fill the earth "as the waters cover the sea" (verse 9, NIV). We are still living in the old age, and Satan is the ruler of our world. The kingdom of our Lord has not yet replaced the kingdom of this world (Rev. 11:15).

\* \* \*

But what about Jesus' statement "If it is by the Spirit of God that I drive out demons, then the kingdom of God has come [*ephthasen*] upon you" (Matt. 12:28, NIV; cf. Luke 11:20)?

When a modern evangelist preaches, "Armageddon is upon us," we do not immediately flee to our cellars. Most of the time Jesus said only that the kingdom "is near" (Mark 1:15; Matt. 4:17; 3:2; 10:7; Luke 10:9-11; 21:31).

Something that is near is not yet fully here.

At the Last Supper Jesus said the kingdom was still future: "I will not drink again from the fruit of the vine until the kingdom of God comes" (Luke 22:18, NIV; cf. Mark 14:25; Matt. 26:29). So the kingdom had not come yet. Therefore, the one statement in Luke 11:20 that the kingdom "has come" must be proleptic and anticipatory.

We find similar terminology in the prophets. Jeremiah 50:31 and 51:13 say the time for the punishment of Babylon "has come" (NIV; LXX: *hekei*); but according to Jeremiah 51:33, 47, this means only that it will *soon* come. In other words, "has come" may mean "is near." "The hour has come" in Mark 14:41 (NIV) stands in parallel with "the time is near" in Matthew 26:45 (HCSB). The two phrases appear back to back in Mark 1:15: "The right time has come! The kingdom of God is near" (NCV).

An instructive parallel to Mark 1:15 is Ezekiel 7:7 (NIV): "The time has come! The day is near!" Ezekiel 7:1-12 repeatedly asserts that the "end" (the destruction of Jerusalem) had arrived for Israel (i.e., it was very near). Just as Ezekiel was telling his audience they were standing on the verge of destruction, Jesus was warning His audience they were standing at the edge of the kingdom; indeed, the King was already among them.

But neither Luke 11:20 or 17:21 can be taken simply to mean that the kingdom is already present because of Luke 22:18: "I will not drink again from the fruit of the vine until the kingdom of God comes" (NIV). The kingdom in which swords were beaten into plowshares and no one had to teach another to know the Lord, and so on, obviously still lay in the future—but in the immediate future, as far as He could see, and so could speak as if it were already a present reality.

If you have any remaining doubt about this, Jesus also says in Mark 3:26 that Satan "has an end" (NKJV). Yet the devil is apparently still with us. Similarly, 2 Timothy 1:10 declares that Jesus has destroyed death. But we still die. Gospel passages that suggest the kingdom has come, then, have the same proleptic sense as statements about the end of death and Satan.

While in many ways the kingdom hasn't come, in some ways it has. A new door stands open in heaven, a new power is at work in the world. During World War II, even before Allied troops liberated German concentration camps, tidings of their proximity had a dramatic effect on guards and prisoners, not always for the better. Likewise, God's Messiah had invaded Satan's kingdom, already setting free some of his captives. Jesus' authority over demons showed that the kingdom was present in penumbra, so near that its effects were intruding into the present age (Heb. 6:5). The powers of hell, if not abolished, had been breached. As far as Jesus was concerned, the new kingdom was unfolding and would soon be consummated. As a movement of faith and fealty, it was already making its way in the world, and people were pressing into it (Matt. 11:12; 21:31; 23:13; Luke 16:16; Mark 12:34).

If all of this is still confusing, then perhaps a parallel in the career of another Jewish messiah, one suggested by N. T. Wright, may be helpful. In the A.D. 130s Bar-Kochba, "son of the star," led the last major uprising of the Jews against Rome.

> Bar-Kochba went so far as to have coins minted, numbering the years from "1", indicating the beginning of his declaration of independence. He behaved toward his followers as though he were already king. But this "inaugurated eschatology" . . . remained in need of a final victory, which never came. If we had asked Bar-Kochba or his followers whether they were living in the time of the kingdom, their very coins—the only real "mass media" of the ancient world—would have answered in the affirmative. Denial would have meant disloyalty. But if we conclude from this that they had no future hope, nothing left to aspire to, that their god had established his kingdom once and for all, we would be ludicrously wrong. Once we think historically, the language of a kingdom present yet future, already established yet needing still to win its decisive victory, makes perfect sense.[5]

We can state the matter in terms of precedents actually known to Jesus. After Rome appointed Herod the Great as king of the Jews, it was three years of fight and flight before Herod could assume the throne in Jerusalem, and then only after waging war against the city and slaughtering his opponents.[6] Before he could reign in peace, Herod had to come "with power" (cf. Mark 9:1; 13:26), that is, in force, with the aid of the Romans under the general Sossius, who made Herod's enemies his footstool.

An even more important precedent than Herod would be the reign of David. In one sense it began the moment Samuel anointed him. Yet, as with Herod, that anointing only inaugurated an era of trouble and persecution. Full kingdom authority arrived only in stages.

First, David was anointed, "and from that day on the Spirit of the Lord came powerfully upon David" (1 Sam. 16:13, NIV). The corresponding event in the life of Jesus would be the baptism by John, when "God anointed Jesus of Nazareth with the Holy Spirit and power" (Acts 10:38, NIV; cf. 4:26, 27; Luke 4:14, 18).

Next, "the men of Judah came to Hebron, and there they anointed David king over the house of Judah" (2 Sam. 2:4, NIV). The corresponding stage in the life of Jesus would perhaps be the disciples' confession of allegiance at Caesarea Philippi (Matt. 16:13-20).

Finally, after the rebels who remained loyal to Saul had been subdued seven years later, "all the tribes of Israel came to David at Hebron" and anointed him king over all Israel (2 Sam. 5:1, NIV). Did Jesus hope that something like that would happen at His triumphal entry into Jerusalem?

At any rate, just as those who did not want David to rule over them delayed his final inauguration, so with the Son of David. His reign began at His ascension. The worldwide power and the glory would materialize soon enough.

So has the kingdom preached by Jesus ever come? Although Jesus reigns in the hearts of His followers, His domain is not universal. If Satan is still the god of this world (2 Cor. 4:4), then the kingdom still awaits consummation. The audience of John the Baptist in Matthew 3:2 and of Jesus in Matthew 4:17 would have understood the kingdom they preached to be the glorious one of Daniel 7 and Isaiah 60-66. That kingdom is yet future.

And that is why Christians still pray, "Thy kingdom come."

---

1. See Tanhuma Ex. 25:3, 4; Pirke de Rabbi Eliezer, trans. Gerald Friedlander (New York: Bloch Pub. Co., 1916), p. 83.

2. Josephus, *Antiquities of the Jews* 10.272-276; 4 Ezra 12; Targum of Jonathan on Hab. 3:17 and Gen. 15:12.

3. E. P. Sanders, *Jesus and Judaism* (Minneapolis: Fortress Press, 1985), p. 152.

4. C. E. B. Cranfield, *A Critical and Exegetical Commentary on the Epistle to the Romans* (New York: T & T Clark, 1979, 2004), vol. 2, p. 861.

5. N. T. Wright, *Jesus and the Victory of God* (Minneapolis: Fortress Press, 1996), p. 468.

6. Josephus, *Antiquities* 14.365-15.10.

# CHAPTER 12

# The Triumphal Entry

In the end of the previous chapter we mentioned the triumphal entry of Jesus into Jerusalem. What was that all about? What was He trying to do?

The Greek term *parousia* denotes a special visit to a city by a dignitary. The triumphal entry was Jesus' first *parousia,* His first "coming."

Ancient protocol required that a dignitary be met outside the city by a delegation, which then escorted the person back inside. We find many examples in Jewish and Roman literature. "When the men were returning home after David had killed the Philistine, the women came out from all the towns of Israel to meet King Saul with singing and dancing, with joyful songs and with timbrels and lyres" (1 Sam. 18:6, NIV). After the death of Absalom, David's subjects went out to meet him at the Jordan and escort him back to the throne (2 Sam. 19:14ff.). After Jonathan, the high priest of the Jews, reached Askalon, "the people of the city came out to meet him with great pomp" (1 Macc. 10:86, NRSV). As the king of Egypt marched into Syria, "the people of the towns opened their gates to him and went out to meet him" (1 Macc. 11:2, NRSV). And when Apollonius visited Jerusalem, "he was welcomed magnificently by Jason [the high priest] and the city, and ushered in with a blaze of torches and with shouts" (2 Macc. 4:22, NRSV; cf. 3:9).

Josephus claims that a procession of priests clothed in fine linen, followed by the citizens wearing white garments and led by the high priest in purple and scarlet, all welcomed Alexander the Great at Jerusalem.[1] He also cites a letter from Antiochus the Great saying that the citizens of Jerusalem "gave us a splendid reception, and met us with their senate."[2] When Vitellius, who ordered Pilate to Rome to answer for his misdeeds, entered Jerusalem at a Passover, he was "magnificently received."[3] Philo says that after Marcus Agrippa had visited Herod in Jerusalem and honored the Temple, the Jews conducted him from city to city back to the coast with branches strewn on the road.[4] Jerusalem had a long history of honoring the "triumphal entry," or *parousia,* of dignitaries.

After the death of Antiochus Epiphanes in the second century B.C., the citizens of Jerusalem, "carrying ivy-wreathed wands and beautiful branches and also fronds of palm," lauded Judas Maccabeus and "offered hymns of thanksgiving to him who had given success to the purifying of his own holy place" (2 Macc. 10:7, NRSV). The parallel in 1 Maccabees 13:41-52 is instructive:

> In the one hundred and seventieth year [142 B.C.] the yoke of the Gentiles was removed from Israel, and the people began to write in their documents and contracts, "In the first year of Simon the great high priest and commander and leader of the Jews." . . . He expelled [the inhabitants of Gazara] from the city and cleansed the houses in which the idols were located, and then *entered it with hymns and praise. He removed all uncleanness from it,* and settled in it those who observed the law. He also strengthened its fortifications and built in it a house for himself. [The Gentile holdouts] who were in the citadel at Jerusalem were prevented from going in and out to buy and sell in the country. So they were very hungry, and many of them perished from famine. Then they cried to Simon to make peace with them, and he did so. But he expelled them from there and *cleansed the citadel from its pollutions.* On the twenty-third day of the second month, in the one hundred seventy-first year, *the Jews entered it with praise and palm branches,* and with harps and cymbals and stringed instruments, and with hymns and songs, because a great enemy had been crushed and removed from Israel. Simon decreed that every year they should celebrate this day with rejoicing (NRSV).

Note that the passage associates both of the two triumphal entrances with the cleansing of some central public edifice. Also observe that the events marked the beginning of Jewish self-rule by the century-long Hasmonean dynasty. The Hasmonean Maccabees, however, could not claim Davidic descent. Imagine, then, how the Passover Jews of Jesus' day would have interpreted something like a reenactment of the Maccabean triumphal entry *by someone known as a son of David.* The crowd sang to Jesus the conqueror's psalm, the same words sung and shouted by the citizens of Jerusalem "when they welcomed back Simon Maccabaeus after he had conquered Acra and wrested it from Syrian dominion more than 100 years before." The people clearly had high hopes that Jesus would lead them in victory over Rome.[5]

The Romans often honored their conquerors by giving them a formal ceremony of honor known as a triumph, a grand and elaborate parade. It was a scene of such intense exuberance as to create a lasting memory. The people would go out to meet the victor, then escort him back to the city. Here are several examples from Plutarch's *Parallel Lives,* in which he describes the triumphal homecomings of several Roman conquerors. When Cicero returned to Rome shortly after the assassination of Julius Caesar, "such multitudes flocked out to meet him, that the compliments and civilities which were paid him at the gates, and at his entrance into the city, took up almost one whole day's time."[6]

Earlier, when Cato the Younger returned to Rome by ship in 56 B.C., "the news did not fail to reach Rome that he was coming up the river. All the magistrates, the priests, and the whole senate, with great part of the people, went out to meet him; both the banks of the Tiber were covered with people; so that his entrance was in solemnity and honor not inferior to a triumph."[7]

In 386 B.C., after Camillus saved Rome from a seven-month siege by the Gauls, the people honored him with a triumph "as he deserved, having saved his country that was lost, and brought the city, so to say, back again to itself. For those that had fled abroad, together with their wives and children, accompanied him as he rode in; and those who had been shut up in the capitol, and were reduced almost to the point of perishing with hunger, went out to meet him, embracing each other as they met, and weeping for joy, and, through the excess of the present pleasure, scarcely believing in its truth."[8]

Before that there was Alcibiades, who returned triumphantly to Athens in 407 B.C.:

> And now Alcibiades began to desire to see his native country again, or rather to show his fellow-citizens a person who had gained so many victories for them. He set sail for Athens. . . . As soon as he was landed, the multitude who came out to meet him scarcely [appeared] to see any of the other captains, but came in throngs about Alcibiades, and saluted him with loud acclamations, and still followed him; those who could press near him crowned him with garlands, and they who could not come up so close yet stayed to behold him afar off, and the old men pointed him out . . . to the young ones. . . . He had raised them up from this low and deplorable condition, and had not only restored them to their ancient dominion of the sea, but had also made them everywhere victorious over their enemies on land. . . . The people being summoned to an assembly, Alcibiades came in amongst them, and . . . [gave the speech recorded here. Afterward] the people crowned him with crowns of gold, and created him general, both at land and sea, with absolute power.[9]

Note the parallels here with the "many crowns" on the head of Jesus in Revelation 19:12, and with Jesus' claim to plenary authority in Matthew 28:18.

Finally, we should compare the military invasion by the armies of heaven described in 1 Thessalonians 4:16, 17 with this description of the advance of Alexander the Great on Babylon. The Babylonians welcomed Alexander as a deliverer, because they hated their Persian masters, who had suppressed the Chaldean religion and destroyed the temple of Belus:

"When Alexander started from Arbela, he advanced straight towards Babylon; and when he was now not far from that city, he drew up his army in order of battle and marched forward. The Babylonians came out to meet him in mass, with their priests and rulers, each of whom individually brought gifts, and offered to surrender their city, citadel, and money. Entering the city, he commanded the Babylonians to rebuild all the temples which Xerxes had destroyed, and especially that of Belus, whom the Babylonians venerate more than any other god."[10]

As the Babylonians came out to greet their deliverer, Alexander, so Jesus' followers will welcome Him when He arrives with the armies of heaven.

Alexander entered Jerusalem itself during the high priesthood of Shimon Ha-Tzaddik (Simon the Just), a high priest who followed Ezra and was known for his piety. The story is told in at least two sources: b. Yoma 69a and Josephus's *Antiquities* (11.325-339). As Alexander approached Jerusalem, Shimon donned the white garments worn on Yom Kippur when he entered the Holy of Holies, and led a delegation out to meet (*hypantesis*) him. Alexander suddenly prostrated himself on the ground before Shimon. When Alexander's puzzled general asked why, he replied that every night before a victory, he would see in a dream a figure that looked exactly like the Jewish high priest, who would advise him on tactics for the following day. And that advice had never failed him. Afterward Shimon gave Alexander a tour of the Temple. Impressed, Alexander requested that a marble image of himself be placed there. Shimon demurred and suggested instead that all babies born that year to priests would be named Alexander, which explains that name among Jewish males.

* * *

Jesus accepted honors reserved for dignitaries and kings. Impersonating a king was no trivial offense in the Roman Empire. And that is exactly what the authorities thought He was doing. It's true that such honors might indeed be accorded to someone whose courageous deed resulted in the salvation of a people or a king, as in the case of Mordecai (Esther 6:6-12) or Judith (Judith 15:8-16:20). When the city of Tiberius submitted to Vespasian, "he then advanced with his army to the city. The population opened their gates to him and went out to meet him with acclamations, hailing him as savior and benefactor." At Vespasian's much grander *parousia* into Rome, the entire population emerged to greet him and hail him as their savior.[11]

But Jesus did not fit the traditional template of a military messiah. He was riding a donkey, the symbol of peace, not a horse, an image of war, in harmony with Zechariah 9:9, 10. This important milestone in the life of Jesus, His *parousia* into Jerusalem, is one of the few events recorded in all four Gospels. The Jerusalem parade was no impromptu celebration. Jesus engineered it Himself. He told His disciples to go looking for the beast on which He rode. His partisans were the Passover visitors from Galilee (John 11:55, 56; 12:12, 13; cf. 4:45). The people of Jerusalem did not seem to know Him (Matt. 21:10, 11) and apparently snubbed Him.

Perhaps a more accurate term here than "triumphal entry" might be "royal entry." Jesus was clearly signaling His royal intentions by accepting honors normally reserved for magistrates. When an earlier crowd had attempted to take Jesus by force and make Him king, He withdrew (John 6:15). His time had not yet arrived (cf. John 7:6, 8). Now when the people called Him "king," He refused to rebuke them (Luke 19:38-40; John 12:13). Immediately preceding the account of the royal entry in Luke is the saying at the end of Jesus' parable of the minas: "Those enemies of mine who did not want me to be king over them—bring them here and kill them in front of me" (Luke 19:27, NIV).

A few days later Jesus confessed under oath that He was the king of the Jews (Mark 15:2; Luke 23:2, 3; John 18:37; 19:12; Acts 17:7), endured mockery from the soldiers for His kingly pretensions (Mark 15:16-20), and *was crucified on the basis of that charge* (verse 26). Only Rome could bestow such a title, so to claim it for oneself was sedition.

Centuries earlier Sanballat had baited Nehemiah with a threatening letter in which he alleged rumors that "the Jews are plotting to revolt," and that "you are about to become their king and have even appointed prophets to make this proclamation about you in Jerusalem: 'There is a king in Judah!'" Nehemiah denied the charge (Neh. 6:6-8, NIV). Even though Artaxerxes had appointed him governor of the region (Neh. 5:14), kingly claims would have amounted to a declaration of independence.

In contrast to Nehemiah, Jesus, who had no formal civic authority at all, confessed at His trial that He was indeed Israel's king. And that was a capital offense.

It is important to recognize that "King of Israel" and "Messiah" are synonymous terms (cf. Mark 15:32: "Christ the King of Israel"). Christ is the English version of the Greek *christos,* which corresponds to the Hebrew word *messiach.* Transliterated "Messiah," it is translated "Anointed One," and may refer to any anointed ruler of Israel (e.g., 1 Sam. 2:10; 16:6; 26:9, 11, 16; 2 Sam. 22:51; 23:1; Lam. 4:20; 2 Chron. 6:42). To claim to be the Christ was to profess to be the king of the Jews (Luke 23:2, 3).

Rome had actually given Herod the Great the title "king of the Jews."[12] However, according to Tacitus, "On Herod's death, one Simon, without waiting for the approbation of the Emperor, usurped the title of king. He was punished by Quintilius Varus then governor of Syria; and the nation, with its liberties curtailed, was divided into three provinces under the sons of Herod."[13] The Romans titled Herod's sons "ethnarch" or "tetrarch" and abolished the designation "king." Herod Antipas, who held office at the time of Jesus' trial, would not have looked kindly on a pretender to a title that had been denied even to him.

Though Rome might allow a ruler over one of the subject provinces to bear the title of king, to assume it without the empire's blessing was sedition. Imagine how contemporary Americans would feel about anyone who proclaimed themselves president for life of the United States. The Romans felt the same way about kings. First Maccabees 8:14 says of the Romans: "Not one of them . . . put on a crown or wore purple as a mark of pride" (NRSV).

In a little-known parallel to Herod's slaughter of the children at Bethlehem, Suetonius tells how the Roman senate dealt with the fearful threat of a newborn king in 63 B.C.: "According to Julius Marathus, a few months before Augustus was born a portent was generally observed at Rome, which gave warning that nature was pregnant with a king for the Roman people; thereupon the Senate in consternation decreed that no male child born that year should be reared; but those whose wives were with child saw to it that the decree was not filed in the treasury, since each one appropriated the prediction to his own family."[14]

Kingly aspirations were hazardous even for Roman rulers. Julius Caesar was assassinated because, having already achieved the title *dictator perpetuo,* he had crowds placing laurel wreaths on his statue and calling him *rex,* king. His supporters then requested the Roman senate to grant him the title. After Julius's death, not even the revered Augustus dared to declare himself king, although he was called god. Herod Antipas, who reigned as tetrarch for 42 years—longer than his father, Herod the Great—was finally deposed in A.D. 39 for the political faux pas of asking the emperor Caligula to make him a king.[15]

What was dangerous even for Roman rulers was most deadly for Jewish peasants: Josephus describes in *Wars of the Jews* the unhappy end of several who declared themselves king during Jesus' infancy.[16]

At first Jesus discreetly refrained from such claims, at least in public: "Jesus warned his followers not to tell anyone he was the Christ" (Matt. 16:20, NCV; cf. Mark 8:29, 30; Luke 4:41; 9:20, 21). When crowds asked if Jesus was the Christ, His answer was never a simple yes (Luke 22:67; John 10:24, 25). In public discussion He coyly broached the topic without actually claiming to be the Christ (Mark 12:35-37; Matt. 22:41-46; 23:10). But in private with His disciples He was more candid (Mark 9:41; Matt. 24:5).

Not until the royal entry did Jesus openly assume a kingly stance. A few days later He admitted under oath to the Jewish rulers that He was the Christ, but then immediately reverted to His favorite title, "Son of man" (Mark 14:61, 62; Matt. 26:63, 64; Luke 22:67-70). To Pilate Jesus made the equivalent admission that He was King of the Jews (Mark 15:2; Matt. 27:11; Luke 23:3; cf. John 18:37), and, as we have already noted, on the basis of that charge the Roman official had Him crucified (Mark 15:26). In effect, He was forced to plead guilty to sedition. Although known for His agility in escaping rhetorical traps, Jesus could not deny who He was.

While the Temple incident with the money changers would have infuriated the Jewish authorities, it was the royal entry that offered grounds for a Roman execution. Jesus was certainly acting like a king. He followed the script of Zechariah 9:9: "Your king comes to you . . . riding on a donkey" (NIV), while the people followed that of the coronation of Psalm 118:26, 27: "Blessed is he who comes in the name of the Lord. From the house of the Lord we bless you. . . . With boughs in hand, join in the festal procession up to the horns of the altar" (NIV). The royal entry resembles earlier Jewish coronation ceremonies: "Our lord King David has made Solomon king. . . . They have put him on the king's mule. . . . From there they have gone up cheering, and the city resounds with it" (1 Kings 1:43-47, NIV). "They quickly took their cloaks and spread them under him on the bare steps. Then they blew the trumpet and shouted, 'Jehu is king!' " (2 Kings 9:13, NIV).

The procession ended at the Temple (Mark 11:11), only to arouse the indignation of the Pharisees (Luke 19:39) and chief priests (Matt. 21:15). Like the skeptics at the inauguration of Saul who cried, "How can this fellow save us?" (1 Sam. 10:27, NIV), they dissented from the Galilean hoi polloi who at the royal entry cried, "Hosanna," which means "O save us" (Mark 11:9). The first son of David, Solomon, also seated on a mule, was anointed by the high priest and announced with trumpets at his coronation (1 Kings 1:38-40). But when Jesus rode into Jerusalem, where were the trumpets and the priests? The authorities disdained what they considered an impostor. The trumpets would have to wait until a future *parousia* (Matt. 24:31).

Brent Kinman cites examples of the *parousia* in Roman literature and argues that Luke presents the so-called triumphal entry of Jesus into Jerusalem actually as the *parousia* of a king, and that the ensuing pronouncement of doom on the lips of Jesus in Luke 19:42-44 implies disappointment with the reception given Him by the Jewish leaders. The welcome Jesus received was hardly fit for a king. The response of Jerusalem to the coming of Jesus would have been seen as "an appalling insult," Kinman states, since the religious and social elite failed to show up.[17] Or as John 1:11 puts it: when Jesus came to His own, His own did not receive Him.

A failure to extend a proper greeting to the visiting dignitary could have grave consequences for a city. When a Samaritan village to whom messengers had been sent refused to welcome Jesus on His way to Jerusalem, the disciples called for their destruction (Luke 9:51-56). Kinman cites the Roman magistrate L. Verginius Rufus, who besieged the city of Vesontio, because it did not receive him properly.[18] The chief priests in Jerusalem urged the crowds to meet the troops of the Roman governor of Judea, Florus, with customary regard, so that he might not have any grounds for further destruction of the city.[19] Another interesting parallel, overlooked by Kinman, is 1 Maccabees 7:33-35:

"After these events Nicanor went up to Mount Zion. Some of the priests of the sanctuary and some of the elders of the people came out to greet him peaceably and to show him the burnt offering that was being offered for the king. But he mocked them and derided them and defiled them and spoke arrogantly, and in anger he swore this oath, 'Unless Judas and his army are delivered into my hands this time, then if I return safely I will burn up this house.' And he went out in great anger" (NRSV).

Just prior to the event the forces of Judas had killed 500 of Nicanor's men in battle and then retreated into Jerusalem. When Nicanor came in after them, at least some of the Jerusalem leaders felt obligated to honor Nicanor's *parousia*. But why was the high priest missing? Nicanor threatens to destroy the Temple unless Judas is turned over to him. The parallel passage in 2 Maccabees 14:33 is interesting: Nicanor "stretched out his right hand toward the sanctuary, and swore an oath: 'If you do not hand Judas over to me as prisoner, I will level this shrine of God to the ground and tear down the altar, and build here a splendid temple to Dionysus' " (NRSV). Compare the words ascribed to Jesus by the witnesses at His trial in Mark 14:58: "I will destroy this temple made with human hands and in three days will build another, not made with hands" (NIV).

Accorded even less honor than Nicanor at his entry into Jerusalem, Jesus shortly thereafter threatened the Temple, too, both by His actions and by citing a passage from Jeremiah that portended its destruction. Was Jesus imitating Nicanor? Or is the parallel mere coincidence? Luke's portrait of Jesus suggests sorrow as opposed to the arrogant pride of Nicanor. At any rate, it is possible to see in Jesus' Temple action a public, if cryptic, signal of His intentions toward the Temple, which He privately disclosed more fully to the disciples on Olivet. And it is significant that what immediately follows is His less-than-triumphal *parousia* into the city. If the events bore any symbolic intent, then they imply an association between the Second Coming and the destruction of Jerusalem.

I believe Jesus designed His actions to lead to a particular end whether or not the Jews accepted Him as King.

We must assume that Jesus was wily (Matt. 10:16) and not naive. Obviously He knew that impersonating a king was a capital offense. So it is hard to avoid the impression that He was intentionally provoking a crisis. S. G. F. Brandon claims that His actions were "obviously calculated to cause the authorities, both Jewish and Roman, to view him and his movement as subversive."[20] His time had come at last (Mark 2:20; 14:41; Matt. 9:15; Luke 5:35; John 12:23; 13:1; 16:21; 17:1). And now that it had, His strategies changed (see, e.g., Luke 22:35-37). If He must die, it would not be in some hidden dungeon, like John the Baptist, but in the most public way possible. Jesus surely suspected His actions would lead to His execution. The Temple cleansing and royal entry were calculated to enrage all parties, Jewish and Roman, forcing the issue and insuring martyrdom.

Jesus knew that He would not come into His kingdom that day, as that was not due until the *end* of the seventieth week, and it was only the middle of that week. According to Daniel 9:26, the Anointed One had to be "cut off" in the middle of the final "week" of years in order to inaugurate the kingdom.

Jesus died either in the year 30 or the year 33. No other date is possible. The debate between these dates occupies many pages on the Internet. But the traditional and still best-supported date for the triumphal entry, known in Christian tradition as "Palm Sunday," is Sunday, April 2, A.D. 30, which is right in the middle of the seven-year "week," or *Shemitah,* or sabbatical period, that began in the fall of the year 26, almost exactly 1,260 days earlier. It was time for Jesus to die, and it was all in God's plan.

So Jesus set His face toward Calvary and the horror of the cross.

1. Josephus, *Antiquities of the Jews* 11.329-332.

2. Ibid., 12.138.

3. Ibid., 18.90.

4. Philo, *De Legatione ad Caium* 297.

5. William Barclay, *The Gospel of John* (Louisville, Ky.: Westminster John Knox Press, 2001), vol. 2, p. 136.

6. Plutarch, *Parallel Lives,* Cicero.

7. Ibid., Cato the Younger.

8. Ibid., Camillus.

9. Ibid., Alcibiades.

10. Arrian, *Anabasis* 3.16.

11. Josephus, *Wars of the Jews* 3.459; 7.63-74.

12. Josephus, *Antiquities* 16.291, 311; 17.92.

13. Tacitus, *Histories* 5.

14. Suetonius, *Lives of the Twelve Caesars,* Augustus 94.

15. John P. Meier, *A Marginal Jew* (New York: Doubleday, 2001), vol. 3, p. 295.

16. Josephus, *Wars* 2.55-65.

17. Brent Kinman, "Parousia, Jesus' 'A-Triumphal Entry, and the Fate of Jerusalem,' " *Journal of Biblical Literature* 118 (1999): 279-294.

18. Dio Cassius 63.24.1.

19. Josephus, *Wars* 2.318-324.

20. S. G. F. Brandon, *Jesus and the Zealots* (Manchester, U.K.: Univ. of Manchester, 1967), p. 324.

# CHAPTER 13

# The Road to Forever

Despondent disciples filled the room. Tears still glistened in the eyes of some, and low voices murmured doubtful sighs as they discussed the great disappointment they had faced only a little more than a day ago. Others showed signs of excitement. Cleopas and his companion were not among the Twelve, but they may have earlier been among the 70. They were probably in the upper room with the disciples that dreary Sunday morning when the women came back with the amazing report that the tomb was empty.

The men did not believe, so Simon Peter ran down to see for himself (Luke 24:12). That afternoon Cleopas and his companion left, as they had a long way to go to Emmaus before it got so dark that they couldn't see the thieves that might be hiding along the way. They may have left before Peter returned. Hopeless and faithless, they began the seven-mile journey toward home.

Who was "Cleopas" (Luke 24:18)?

It seems that Jesus' adoptive father Joseph had a brother by the name of Clopas. In that culture he would have taken Jesus under his wing after Joseph died, which, according to tradition, he did early on.

John 19:25 claims that "near the cross of Jesus stood his mother, his mother's sister, Mary the wife of Clopas, and Mary Magdalene" (NIV).

Many scholars believe that Clopas/Cleopas/Cleophas are the same man. The famous church historian Eusebius, who wrote about A.D. 324, states that after the death of James (about A.D. 62), "those of the apostles and disciples of the Lord that were still living came together from all directions with those that were related to the Lord according to the flesh (for the majority of them also were still alive) to take counsel as to who was worthy to succeed James. They all with one consent pronounced Symeon, the son of Clopas, of whom the Gospel also makes mention; to be worthy of the episcopal throne of that parish. He was a cousin, as they say, of the Saviour. For Hegesippus records that Clopas was a brother of Joseph."[1]

Let's assume, then, that Cleopas and Clopas are the same person, as many scholars do, and that he was Jesus' uncle.

So who was the second disciple? Who would Cleopas be traveling to Emmaus with? Here are the three leading candidates.

First, it may have been Luke. The fact that he and only he recorded the story suggests that he was an eyewitness. But then, of course, he may also have heard the details from another eyewitness.

Hippolytus of Rome wrote a document about A.D. 200 called "On the Seventy Apostles of Christ." Now, Hippolytus was a disciple of Irenaeus, who was a disciple of Polycarp, who was a disciple of the apostle John. In his book Hippolytus claims that Luke, along with Mark, was one of the 70 "other" disciples sent out in Luke 10—another story recorded only by Luke. In fact, he even states that both Luke and Mark had previously turned away from Jesus, like many others mentioned in John 6:66, after they heard the shocking sermon of John 6. Here is what Hippolytus wrote:

"These two belonged to the seventy disciples who were scattered by the offence of the word which Christ spoke, 'Except a man eat my flesh, and drink my blood, he is not worthy of me.' But the one being induced to return to the Lord by Peter's instrumentality, and the other by Paul's, they were honored to preach that gospel on account of which they also suffered martyrdom, the one being burned, and the other being crucified on an olive tree."

But many scholars doubt Hippolytus's list of the 70. And if Hippolytus is not correct, then Luke was not one of the 70 and may not have even known Jesus personally. And even if Hippolytus is correct, then the sending out of the 70 would have had to be prior to the events of John 6, which seems unlikely; but more important, if Luke was not induced to return to Jesus until after the conversion of Paul, then he would not have been on the road to Emmaus.

That leaves us with two other candidates: Cleopas' son Symeon, or his wife Mary, which would explain why Luke only mentions one of the two of them. Let's assume it was Mary, one of the women around the cross.

The pair had just experienced the most wrenching weekend of their lives. Now entirely spent, they wound their way home from an exhausting Passover trip as the shadows grew long.

The road to Emmaus from Jerusalem is a strenuous hike of about seven miles. It winds uphill and down. About a mile from Jerusalem begins a dreary wasteland of barren rocks, down into a valley where there is water, then a slippery path uphill to a very steep pass, then downhill into the Wady Hanina, then uphill to Emmaus, which was somewhere on the overlook.

But they were not just weary. Events had also exhausted their emotional reserves. Their Messiah was dead. They could hardly muster the energy to go on. No doubt they prayed for God to be with them and to protect them from robbers. And from time to time they fell into conversation. Let's use a little homiletical license for a moment and eavesdrop on their conversation:

"How could we have been so wrong?" Cleopas shook his head. "He worked miracles! And yet . . ."

"Someday we'll understand, husband," Mary said.

"But He was . . . so different! From a youngster He was special."

"Yes. You remember His little carvings when He was just a youth?" she asked.

"Yes. He gave me one—the dove. So clever."

"He had a way with animals," Mary continued. "I remember He used to collect them. One day I caught Him preaching to them." She laughed, then her face fell back to weary defeat.

"He collected tools to work in wood and stone. Remember that?"

"Why do you suppose He left behind His craft to found a commune?"

"Well, I think He felt called to it, I guess. But He never brought a woman over to the house. I wondered about that."

"*Mmmm.* Just not interested in marriage. And even when He was building homes, He seemed to have a one-track mind. And it wasn't for building. It was for God. Always studying. Always praying."

"Yes, His heart always had a place for God. So why didn't God have a place for Him? But the hidden things belong to Him. We cannot question the all-wise One. Still, I can hardly bear it. Such a sweet boy. He didn't deserve this." She paused in a grimace of grief. "I remember the times He ate at our house after His father died. There was a certain . . . joy about Him." She paused. "You remember that little thing He did with His hands when He lifted up the bread to God and blessed Him for providing the food."

"Yes, I remember."

They walked for a while in silence, picking their way confidently over the rocky path.

"He was such a powerful prophet," Cleopas said finally. "He proved Himself by His wonderful deeds. He was another John the Baptist. But I suppose His work was finished."

"How could men be so cruel?"

"Those men are appointed by Rome—they love money. They don't love God."

"Where do you suppose His body is now? Did the Romans steal it? Some of my friends claimed the tomb is empty!" his wife exclaimed.

"No, Mary. Wishful thinking. Women's minds play tricks on them. The tomb is sealed, and no one would rob a tomb owned by Joseph of Arimathea."

"Yes, but I've heard that He said He would rise again—"

"Mary, He's dead. Let it go."

They plodded on with downcast faces. They must have been thinking something like, *Since this holy Man, who seemed to work with the power of God, has turned out to be under God's curse, then who can we believe? Whom can we trust? What is right, and what is wrong? Where can we turn?*

How many thousands of God's children have had their hopes dashed by what at the time seems like ignominious defeat. But God always has a hidden plan! The cross is the ultimate example of God disguising His delicious victories as a catastrophe.

* * *

Suddenly a stranger walked with them. "What are you talking about?" he asks.

"Haven't you heard the things that happened in Jerusalem over the weekend?" they reply.

"What things?"

"Jesus the mighty prophet was crucified! And we thought He would redeem Israel. In addition, some of our women have amazed us. When they went to the tomb early this morning they didn't find His body. They came and told us that they had seen a vision of angels, who said He was alive. Then some of our companions went to the tomb and found it just as the women had said, but they did not see Jesus."

For decades after the Resurrection the early church leaders must have wondered why God did something so ridiculous as to appear first to them. That would never do. No one would believe. "From women let no evidence be accepted," writes Josephus, "because of the levity and temerity of their sex."[2]

Why couldn't God show Himself first to a man?

Yet today one of the strongest arguments for the Resurrection is that the women saw it first. You see, no man of that time making up a story would have written it that way. It can't be fiction, so it must be true!

God uses the weak things of this world to confound the strong.

In Luke 24:25 Jesus said to the weary travelers, "How foolish you are, and how slow to believe all that the prophets have spoken!" (NIV).

Have you ever noticed that Jesus was not good at stroking people's egos? He wasn't much for compliments. Paul was actually much better about this. Prophets just aren't very gentle sometimes. Notice what Jesus said to the man who asked for healing for his son: "O faithless and twisted generation, how long am I to be with you and bear with you?" (Luke 9:41, ESV). He once called Peter "Satan." Jesus was a prophet (Matt 21:11; Mark 6:4; Luke 24:19), and when the status quo is far removed from God's ideal, prophets burn with zeal to correct it.

Then the Stranger said, " 'Did not the Messiah have to suffer these things and then enter his glory?' And beginning with Moses and all the Prophets, he explained to them what was said in all the Scriptures concerning himself" (Luke 24:26, 27, NIV).

What passages did Jesus cite that day that proved that the Messiah would be raised from the dead? I have never heard the question answered convincingly.

The two explicit prophecies of the death of the Messiah in the Old Testament are Daniel 9:26, "The Anointed One will be put to death" (NIV), and Zechariah 13:7, "Awake, sword, against my shepherd, against the man who is close to me! . . . Strike the shepherd, and the sheep will be scattered" (NIV). The best commentary on "the man who is close to me" is Jeremiah 30:21: "Their leader will be one of their own; their ruler will arise from among them. I will bring him near and he will come close to me" (NIV). A "shepherd" is a king or leader (cf. Zech. 11; 2 Sam. 5:2; 7:7; Ps. 78:71). Scripture uses the term of the future ideal Davidic king in Ezekiel 34:23; 37:24; and Micah 5:4. Thus Zechariah 13:7 clearly speaks of the death of the coming anointed ruler of Israel. Jesus applied this prophecy to Himself in Mark 14:27 and Matthew 26:31.

From there Jesus could have taken them to Isaiah 53:3: "He was despised and rejected by mankind" (NIV); and verse 7: "He was oppressed and afflicted, yet he did not open his mouth; He was led like a lamb to the slaughter" (NIV). Then He would have cited verses 8-12, which prophesy of His victory over the grave.

Actually, Isaiah 53 never mentions the *messiach,* or Anointed One. Instead the subject is the "Servant of Yahweh," repeatedly identified with Israel in Isaiah 41:8, 9; 43:10; 44:1, 2, 21; 45:4; 48:20; and 49:3. Even Luke 1:54 retains this correlation. But remember: Jesus was Israel. And since Isaiah 49:5-9 clearly distinguishes the Servant from Israel, it is natural to understand Isaiah 42:1-4; 49:5-9; and 52:11-53:12 as speaking of an individual. Whatever the original intent of the passage, even the Jewish Targums of Jesus' day apply it to the Messiah.

Now it gets harder.

He may have pointed to Psalm 71:20: "You will restore my life again; from the depths of the earth you will again bring me up" (NIV). The passage that immediately follows this, Psalm 72, is a Messianic prophecy that promises the son of David universal honor and eternal kingdom.

In 2 Samuel 7:12, LXX, God promised David: "I will raise up [*anastaso*, resurrect] your seed after you, even your own issue, and I will establish his kingdom." I suspect, along with N. T. Wright, that Jesus applied that promise to Himself.

Then there is Jeremiah 37:8, 9, LXX: "In that day, said the Lord, I will break the yoke off their neck, and will burst their bonds, and they shall no longer serve strangers: but they shall serve the Lord their God; and I will raise up [or resurrect, *anastaso*] to them David their king."

Notice the promise in Deuteronomy 18:15, 18 (Septuagint version), cited in Acts 3:22, that God would "raise up" (*anastaso*) a prophet like Moses.

It is likely that Jesus went on to combine those passages with Hosea 6:3, LXX: "in the third day we shall arise [*exanastasi*, as in Philippians 3:11] and live before him." Such passages would be the basis for Jesus' faith in who He was and the certainty of His resurrection from death.

Maybe Jesus quoted to them Zechariah 12:10: "Then I will pour out a spirit of grace and prayer on the house of David and the residents of Jerusalem, and they will look at Me whom they pierced. They will mourn for Him as one mourns for an only child and weep bitterly for Him as one weeps for a firstborn" (HCSB).

As they listened to the voice of this Stranger, hope began to shed its rays through the dark corners of their souls once again. They began to suspect that what they had taken as the end of hope was just the beginning of it. When they saw the event through the eyes of Jesus, it became transformed from a dark tragedy to a sweet triumph. Jesus took the fact that what they had understood as the death knell to faith and showed them from Scripture that it was actually the foundation of faith. Their disappointment was God's appointment. And their great misfortune was their great fortune.

Suddenly they saw it all. Dark things that Jesus had told His inner circle and that had then circulated in the community of followers now made sense. New vistas of understanding dawned. The Messiah had to suffer to atone for sin.

\* \* \*

What happened next shows the courtesy of Jesus, who never imposed on people. "As they approached the village to which they were going, Jesus continued on as if he were going farther. But they urged him strongly, 'Stay with us, for it is nearly evening; the day is almost over.' So he went in to stay with them" (Luke 24:28, 29, NIV).

Notice the pattern: He continued on as if He were going farther. God behaves like this all through Scripture. "He saw the disciples straining at the oars, because the wind was against them. Shortly before dawn he went out to them, walking on the lake. He was about to pass by them" (Mark 6:48, NIV).

John 1:36 says that John the Baptist saw Jesus passing by, and said, "Look, the Lamb of God!" (NIV). What if John had said nothing?

In Genesis 19:2 Lot invited the two strangers to spend the night in his house. " 'No,' they answered, 'we will spend the night in the square' " (NIV). But he insisted. They turned out to be angels.

Then in Genesis 32:26 Jacob's divine antagonist said, " 'Let me go, for it is daybreak.' But Jacob replied, 'I will not let you go unless you bless me' " (NIV).

Jesus always seems to be trying to get away, to pass us by. But He is testing us to see if we really want Him. We must implore Him to come in, must beg for His presence and His power. He does not give Himself to the casual seeker. But to those who compel Him, to those who persist in seeking Him, He will come in, and sup with them.

Jesus has all power in heaven and earth, so it's a good thing that He does not impose Himself where He is not wanted. If you tell Him to leave you alone, He will.

At one of my first churches the senior pastor asked me to visit an Adventist woman who wanted to recover her love for God. Years ago she had been sleeping with someone who was not her husband, and the voice of conscience continued to beckon her back to God. Finally she told God quite emphatically to leave her alone!

And He did! Never again did she feel any pang of conscience or the sense of God's grace in her life. Now she wanted to know how to come back. A long succession of ministers before me had dealt with her and told her she need but say the word, and God would forgive and receive her. They told her—and so did I—that the very fact that she sought help was evidence that she was not forever lost. We talked at length and prayed together. But nothing seemed to help. All I know is what she told me: she never felt God's presence again. She knew something was missing, and she longed for the communion she once had. I trust that she has now at last found the peace of Jesus' presence.

Never tell God to leave you alone! No, tell Him to bother you, to harass you, to use you up, to pour you out, to do whatever He wants with you, to never give up on you or let you go.

So Jesus made as if He would go on. That was the correct protocol, proper etiquette, for such an occasion. But Cleopas and Mary were hospitable people. They were not forgetful to entertain strangers, and in so doing they entertained the Lord of glory Himself. Think of what they might have missed had they not been willing to share their humble table with this Stranger.

When is the last time you had Jesus at your table? Let me ask the question another way. When is the last time you invited someone over to your house? The last time you entertained strangers? Or church leaders? Jesus said, "Inasmuch as you did it to the least of these My brethren, you did it to Me" (NKJV).

When someone needs help, don't pass them by. That's a good way to find Jesus. And if He seems to be passing you by, then just remember: He's tantalizing you, teasing you with opportunity. Wanting to be wanted, He hopes that you will cry out:

"Pass me not, O gentle Savior,
Hear my humble cry;
While on others Thou art calling,
Do not pass me by."

So Cleopas and Mary enjoyed table fellowship with the King of kings and Lord of lords. And Scripture says that "when he was at the table with them, he took bread, gave thanks, broke it and began to give it to them. Then their eyes were opened and they recognized him, and he disappeared from their sight" (Luke 24:30, 31, NIV).

It is unlikely that Jesus bowed His head and asked God to "bless this food." More likely He looked up to heaven, as in Mark 6:41, and offered a blessing over the bread, thanking God for the food. Perhaps Jesus lifted the bread up to heaven, offering it back to God, with a certain flourish.

But what were those wounds in His hands? In a moment of insight they knew that they were with Jesus. But before they could even so much as fall down and worship, He was gone.

"Mary, did you see it? Did you see the way He held His hands when He broke the bread?"

"I saw it! Only one person ever did that! I can't believe it."

"Woman, what did I tell you, He's alive."

"But you said—"

"Oh, that was miles ago. Forget that! My heart was burning while He explained the Scriptures on the way. I knew something special was happening. He's alive! We've gotta go back and tell the others!"

Suddenly life is transformed. Tiredness all gone. Hunger forgotten. Energy restored. The night is young! Let's get going! Places to go, people to tell!

The food grew cold on the table as the two dashed out of the house, full now of new hope, back down the long road to Jerusalem. They had just received the greatest news of their life, and they had to share it. Together they set out running.

Before they were on the road to Emmaus. Now they were on the road to forever.

And where was Jesus now, as the revived pair raced back over the rough ground? He was still with them, delighting in their delight. The unseen bodyguard, He walked beside them, just enjoying the moment. What fun to play hide-and-seek with these people whom He loved. At Jerusalem He passed invisibly through the door and, hidden, listened as the others received the news.

Sometimes we feel the presence of Jesus, sometimes He seems a million miles away. But feelings are unreliable. If we are His, He is always there, weeping with us, laughing with us, walking with us, sitting with us as we type on our computers or dial up our friends. He is the hidden Stranger, there behind the dim unknown, standing deep within the shadows, keeping watch above His own.

When the pair got back to Jerusalem, they found the disciples. By now Peter had returned, and the disciples were already exclaiming, " 'It is true! The Lord has risen and has appeared to Simon.' Then the two told what had happened on the way, and how Jesus was recognized by them when he broke the bread" (Luke 24:34, 35, NIV).

Evidently, though, some still didn't believe. We know this because we get the same story in *Reader's Digest* form in Mark 16:12, 13: "Afterward Jesus appeared in a different form to two of them while they were walking in the country. These returned and reported it to the rest; but they did not believe them either" (NIV). Luke read Mark, and decided to research this story and fill it out.

So Jesus said, "I guess I'm going to have to show up Myself." And suddenly He was among them.

"Shalom!" He said.

"It's a ghost!" they cried.

"Don't be silly," He smiled. "See My hands and feet? Ghosts don't have flesh and bones. Here, give Me some fish to eat. Everybody knows ghosts don't eat."

Jesus gave His apostles ample evidence that He was alive—two separate appearances and many eyewitnesses, Simon Peter earlier, and now Cleopas and his friend, and then He added the empirical evidence of His bodily presence. Eventually more than 500 people saw Him alive (1 Cor. 15:6)!

Today we don't have the bodily presence, but we still have the testimony of those who saw and touched Him. And that's enough. It is unreasonable not to believe on the basis of abundant eyewitness testimony. After all, almost everything we know is based on hearsay. The moon landing? World War II? The atomic bomb? The existence of China? To most of us, it's all hearsay. We weren't there. Life is like that. Ninety-nine percent of what we believe we personally cannot prove, but we believe because somebody says so. The Resurrection is no different.

The one thing that should never be mere hearsay is the presence of Jesus in our hearts, and the story of what He has done for us. That's our testimony.

* * *

God still comes to us in disguise, as to the two on the road to Emmaus, or as a ghost to the disciples on the Lake of Galilee. To some He draws near in the darkness of an illness, or in an accident that is physically and emotionally crippling. He comes to us in some misfortune, some loss, some Gethsemane, and uses it to turn our lives in a direction of glory and puts us on the road to forever.

Bill Spangler was an honest welder and an ornery farmer who would take after cattle with a pitchfork to get them to mind. But tragedy brought a great divide in his life. God turned the death of one into life for many.

One day in 1974 Bill got word that his eldest son, Gary, 17, had died suddenly when his car hit an abutment. Blinded by tears, Bill sped toward Hagerstown, pulling to the roadside when he realized he was driving 95 mph.

God suddenly reached out and touched him. He heard a voice ask, "What are you doing?"

"How can I go on living?" he replied.

"Now you know what it cost Me when I gave My Son for you," the voice told him.

Spangler decided to devote part of his life to sharing God's love and forgiveness.

He began volunteering on Sundays at the Maryland Correctional Training Center. And for the next 40 years he gave talks, Bible studies, and loved those prisoners. And they loved him back.

When he died in 2011, I conducted his funeral. He had been married to the same woman for 74 years. Bill was responsible for a rather large tribe of descendants: 8 children; 5 foster children; 30 grandchildren; 68 great-grandchildren; and 23 great-great-grandchildren. That means he had grandchildren who had grandchildren.

But his spiritual children outnumbered them all. During the 38 years of his prison ministry he was responsible for nearly 300 baptisms. He never stopped going to the prison until it became physically impossible for him to get there.

Through the years Bill won several awards for his service from the state. But his greatest reward is yet to come.

---

1. Eusebius, *Church History* 3.11.
2. Josephus, *Antiquities of the Jews* 4.219.